Haunted
Nevada

Haunted Nevada

Ghosts and Strange Phenomena of the Silver State

Janice Oberding
Illustrations by Marc Radle

STACKPOLE
BOOKS

Published by
STACKPOLE BOOKS
5067 Ritter Road
Mechanicsburg, PA 17055
www.stackpolebooks.com

Printed in the United States of America

10 9 8 7 6 5 4 3 2 1

FIRST EDITION

Cover design by Tessa J. Sweigert

Library of Congress Cataloging-in-Publication Data

Oberding, Janice.
  Haunted Nevada : ghosts and strange phenomena of the silver state / Janice
Oberding. — FIRST EDITION.
    pages cm
  Includes bibliographical references.
  ISBN 978-0-8117-1238-5 (pbk.)
  1. Ghosts—Nevada. 2. Haunted places—Nevada. I. Title.
  BF1472.U6O2384 2013
  133.109793—dc23
                            2013019499

To my husband, Bill,
for all his help in this and my other projects.

Contents

Contents

Introduction

THERE ARE THOSE WHO BELIEVE THAT THE VERY WORD "GHOST" IS A misnomer. They argue that a ghost should be called a "spirit" because the spirit is the only thing that survives here on the earthly plane after death. It's probably just a matter of semantics. Think of Shakespeare's *Romeo and Juliet* and the words of the love-struck Juliet:

What's in a name? That which we call a rose
By any other name would smell as sweet.

Ghosts, phantoms, apparitions, spirits, shades—or whatever else one might choose to call them—may walk among us. And why do we believe this? Let me answer that question with another question: how do we explain the fact that nearly every world language contains a word for ghost? Apparently ghosts, or some sort of supernatural phenomenon, are universal.

Here in Nevada, the ghosts come from vastly different backgrounds, reflecting the state's long and colorful history. Nevada was "battle born" during the midst of the Civil War in 1864, when Abraham Lincoln helped it secure statehood. Lincoln had good reason for championing Nevada: the state's lucrative silver mines and its antislavery views made it a valuable addition to the Union cause. A painting of the sixteenth president hangs in a prominent place at the Governor's Mansion in Carson City as a reminder of Nevadans' gratitude.

Most of Nevada lies within the Great Basin region, which also encompasses parts of California, Utah, and Wyoming. During his exploration of the region from 1842 to 1845, army captain and explorer John C. Fremont called the area "the Great Basin" because of its inward drainage (meaning the surface waters drain inward to lakes and rivers, rather than to the ocean).

Water is a precious commodity in Nevada. There is too little water and few resources beyond the precious metals of gold, silver, and copper. Most of the state is part of a dry desert region where little grows save sagebrush, cheat grass, and Joshua trees. And yet, Nevada seemingly has everything—except the ocean, of course. That wasn't always the case: Nevada was home to an ancient sea, as demonstrated by the Ichthyosaur fossils at Berlin-Ichthyosaur State Park. And let's not forget the fabulously crystal-clear Lake Tahoe.

Las Vegas is the state's largest city, but Virginia City is probably the most haunted. Leave the cities and drive a few miles out into any of Nevada's deserts and you'll discover land that seems untouched by time, land that remains much as it has for centuries. Among the sagebrush and the Joshua trees are the remnants of forgotten towns. And in these ghost towns are some ghosts, just as surely as there are ghosts in Las Vegas, Reno, and Lake Tahoe.

Ghosts and their stories have existed since the beginning of time. However, not every ghost story ends in a miraculous discovery and proof of these spirits' existence. Those who research and investigate ghosts know that there are far more questions concerning the whys and hows of ghostly existence than there are answers.

Much like a good road trip, half the fun is in getting there. So it is with ghosts. Half the fun is in the exploring and pondering the possibilities. Ghosts are everywhere, and Nevada is believed to have its share. The stories began with the state's original inhabitants, who believed supernatural forces created the land's rugged and surreal landscape.

Pueblo Grande de Nevada

Las Vegas is young, as least as far as cities go. The former railroad town rose up to be the glamorous gambling mecca that it is today thanks in part to twentieth-century mobster Benjamin "Bugsy" Siegel. The debonair gangster came to town in the 1940s and recognized its money-making potential. The rest, as they say, is history.

Visitors from out of state often come to Las Vegas thinking the region is all new and upstart. When compared with historic buildings on the East Coast dating back to the late seventeenth and early eighteenth centuries, it may seem so. But one must go beyond the gaudy hotel-casinos of the Strip. Just sixty-five miles northeast of Las Vegas, under the waters of Lake Mead, are the remains of an ancient civilization. This mysterious site, which may date back to 8,000 BC, has baffled archaeologists since its discovery.

Anasazi is a Navajo word meaning "ancient ones." Archaeologists know that these early people lived in an area of the Moapa Valley a thousand years ago. They made utilitarian baskets woven from yucca plants and willows. Until they developed the more effective bows and arrows, they used a primitive weapon known as an atlatl, or spear thrower, to hunt game. Over time, the Anasazi explored the use of clay, rather than plants, for their cooking and tool-making needs. They were the area's first farmers and miners. Their staple crops included corn, cotton, and beans. They mined turquoise and salt. That much is known. What the archaeologists don't know is why the Anasazi left the area so abruptly or where they settled once they left the Moapa Valley.

Nothing was known of this lost civilization until 1826, when trailblazer Jedediah Smith and his party discovered salt caves and other relics in what is now southern Nevada. On July 12, 1827, Smith wrote of his find to famed explorer William Clark, then the superintendent of Indian affairs:

> The Paiutes have a number of marble pipes, one of which I obtained and sent to you. Although it has been broken since I have had it in my possession; they told me there was a quantity of the same material south of their country. I also obtained a knife of flint, which I send you, but it has likewise been broken by accident.

Nearly a hundred years after Jedediah Smith's discovery, brothers Fay and John Perkins stumbled upon an archaeological wonder while prospecting for gold in a remote area of the southern Nevada desert in 1924. Anyone else might have plundered the site and forgotten it. Not the Perkins brothers. They rushed back to their homes in nearby Overton to contact Nevada governor James Scrugham, who as a former state engineer realized the importance of the Perkinses' find. But outside help would be needed to properly study and evaluate the site. Scrugham asked archaeologist M. R. Harrington of New York's Heye Foundation to come to Nevada and do the study. As news leaked out about the ruins found in southern Nevada, imaginations stirred and people flocked to the state. The world was fascinated with archaeology and the secrets that could be discovered, especially following the discovery of the tomb of King Tutankhamen two years earlier in Egypt.

The Nevada site was nearly six miles square and was called Pueblo Grande de Nevada; others refer to it as the Lost City. As the dig proceeded, Harrington and his team unearthed walls and floors of communal houses, discovering weapons, tools, and skeletal remains. What they found dispelled previously held myths about the Native Americans who had lived in this region. But this wasn't going to be something they could excavate at their leisure. Time was running out to learn the secrets of Pueblo Grande de Nevada.

Two years earlier, in 1922, the Reclamation Service (the forerunner of the U.S. Bureau of Reclamation) had presented a report calling for the development of a dam on the Colorado that would control floods and serve as a source of hydroelectric power. That same year the Colorado River Compact was agreed upon and signed by seven states including Nevada. The Boulder Canyon Project, also known as the Hoover Dam, was becoming a reality.

According to the Reclamation Service's plans, the Colorado would be dammed at a point roughly thirty miles southeast of Las Vegas, creating a massive reservoir (today's Lake Mead). The Lost City was included in the area that would be inundated, meaning the city truly would be lost forever beneath the lake's waters.

Not all artifacts were lost when the floodwaters rushed in. Those that could be salvaged are now housed at the Lost City Museum in

Overton. The museum, which owns one of the largest collections of the early Southwest people, was built in 1935 for the purpose of displaying the relics of the Lost City's Anasazi. There are also replica adobe pueblos on the museum grounds. Over the years, some people have reported hearing disembodied chanting near some of the displays. There have also been numerous sightings of ancient people in the areas of the pueblos.

Pyramid Lake, Curses, Water Babies, and Stone Mother

Explorer John C. Fremont became the first white person to discover Pyramid Lake, a remnant of prehistoric Lake Lahontan, during his 1844 expedition of the Great Basin. He was favorably impressed with the lake's rugged beauty:

> Beyond a defile between the mountain descended rapidly 2,000 feet; and filling up all the lower space, was a sheet of green water some twenty miles broad. It broke upon our eyes like the ocean . . . we camped on the shore, opposite a very remarkable rock in the lake. It rose, according to our estimate about 600 feet above the water, and from the point we viewed it, presented a pretty exact outline of the great pyramid of Cheops. Like other rocks along the shore, it seemed to be incrusted with calcareous cement. This striking feature suggested a name for the lake, and I called it Pyramid Lake.

There are many legends and stories surrounding Pyramid Lake, which is located thirty miles north of Reno on the Paiute Tribe's Pyramid Lake Reservation. A large sucker fish found in the lake, known as Cui-ui, is found nowhere else on earth. There were tales of an underwater tunnel that led from Pyramid Lake to a similar lake in Africa. There, so the story went, one could find the Cui-ui. According to another story, the lake is home to mysterious "water babies," small, serpentlike creatures that mimic the cries of babies to attract the attention of the unwary. Another version of the water baby story has a young Paiute man venturing to the ocean only to fall in love with a mermaid. When he brought her home to his

family, they demanded he return her to the sea. This broke his heart and infuriated his mermaid, who promptly put a curse on the lake.

Stone Mother is the large rock that resembles a sitting woman. She is said to be a young woman who met and married the ruler of the lake. Over the years the couple had many children. Kids being kids, the siblings didn't always get along. Their arguments were loud and annoying. To maintain harmony the man decided to separate his children, sending them in all different directions. Their mother was so devastated at losing her children that she sat down near a mountain and cried. Her tears became Pyramid Lake.

Those curious people who hear babies crying sometimes venture too near the water's edge and are pulled into the depths of the salty water, never to be seen again. Several people have drowned in the dangerous and unpredictable waters of Pyramid Lake. Many of the bodies of these drowning victims are never recovered. The lake never gives up its dead.

Reno and Lake Tahoe

Reno, the "Biggest Little City in the World," was Nevada's original Sin City. Long before Las Vegas became the state's gambling center, savvy Reno entrepreneurs were raking in the cash in gaming clubs along Center Street, Virginia Street, and Commercial Row.

The city along the Truckee River was founded in 1868. For much of its early existence, it served as a gateway for prospectors and other hopefuls heading to the silver fields around Virginia City. But Reno really came into its own in the early twentieth century, starting in 1931 when Nevada legalized gambling. After the state loosened its divorce laws in 1934, the city quickly became known as the Divorce Capital of the World. Suddenly the little western town near the Sierra was the symbol of all things naughty: nightlife fun, gambling, and quickie divorces.

Nearby Lake Tahoe, noted for its clarity, is one of the world's most beautiful lakes. Tahoe straddles the Nevada–California border, and the two states share oversight of the waters. Its deepest point is 1,645 feet, making it the second-deepest lake in the United States. When looking at the crystal-blue waters of Tahoe on a cloudless spring afternoon, it's difficult to conjure up images of anything ghostly—but it certainly is there.

Lynching at the Wedding Ring Bridge

Many ghost researchers believe violent death leads to a haunting. This may be the reason that Luis Ortiz is said to haunt downtown Reno's Wedding Ring Bridge. Ortiz was a ranch hand who liked to drink, and he was a vicious drunk who turned dangerous after a few whiskeys. In July 1891 he stopped in at a downtown saloon with his month's pay. It wasn't too many drinks later that Ortiz found himself in the middle of a heated argument with three men. The odds were seemingly stacked against him until Ortiz pulled a knife and severely wounded all three of his opponents.

For his part in the melee, Ortiz was convicted of assault and urged by Constable Dick Nash to leave town. He did, at least temporarily. Unfortunately, Ortiz decided to return to Reno two months later.

Ortiz was back in town on the evening of September 17. Angrily brushing past friends who urged him to leave, he headed straight for the bar at the Grand Central Hotel on the corner of Plaza and Virginia Streets. The train ride had left him dry. He spent several hours at the Grand Central swilling whiskey and itching for a fight. Shortly before midnight the owner of the hotel started closing the bar. Ortiz asked about a room and was told that none were available. Taking pity on him, the kindly bartender offered to share his room with the young ranch hand. But Ortiz suddenly grew angrier; he insisted that he wasn't tired, and that he'd come to town to drink and have a good time. He stomped out onto the building's front porch and drew his gun.

"I want to kill some son of a bitch!" he snarled as he pulled the trigger. A bystander was struck in the buttock. Everyone on the porch scattered. No one wanted to get into a gunfight with Ortiz; his reputation was well known to the denizens of this part of town.

When Constable Nash received word that Ortiz was back in town and also drunk, he took two men and headed for the Grand Central. Ortiz had had his chance. This time he was going to jail.

Nash walked to the porch and stared at Ortiz a moment. "C'mon Luis, you're going to jail," he said softly. Without a word, Ortiz raised his gun and fired and then stumbled onto the street. All three officers pounced on him and wrestled him to the ground.

Only when a sharp pain seared through his stomach did Nash realize he was shot. Friends helped him to the home of a doctor, while others hauled Ortiz to jail. The next morning local newspaper reporters came to Ortiz's jail cell where he told them, "I don't know what I did. I was drunk yesterday, all day. I don't know nothing. I don't know who brought me here, or why I was arrested."

Hope for Nash's recovery dimmed when the doctor announced that his wounds were probably fatal. Friends of the fallen constable were outraged. Luis Ortiz was not going to get away with harming their friend.

A secret vigilante group known as the 601 decided to take matters into its own hands. Like groups of the same name in Virginia City and Carson City, Reno's posse was composed of several prominent male citizens who sought to keep their community safe and free of violence. While other citizens of Reno slept soundly in their beds, a clandestine meeting of the 601 was called to order and the problem of Ortiz was quickly resolved. It was decided that he must swing for his transgression. The group marched to the jailhouse and roused Deputy John Caughlin, who was sleeping on a small cot by the door.

"Who's there?" Caughlin asked.

"A friend wants to see you," came the reply.

When the deputy naively opened the door, the angry mob rushed in and overcame him. Ortiz was wakened and told, "You are wanted downtown!" The group stealthily marched their prisoner to the Virginia Street Bridge, which spanned the Truckee River.

"Do you have any final requests?" someone asked Ortiz as the rope was looped around his neck.

"A priest and a glass of water."

A man proffered a whiskey flask. "Whiskey's all we have, Ortiz." Ortiz gulped it down. After explaining where he wished his personal effects to be sent, he faced the mob. "Ready," he announced firmly. The noose was tightened, and Luis Ortiz was hoisted out of this world and into the next.

Five hours later the body was cut down from the bridge. It was too late for Ortiz but not for Constable Nash; within the week he made a full recovery, thus demonstrating how hastily the vigilantes had acted. The *Weekly Gazette Stockman* had this to say about the affair, which was the first and only lynching in Reno's history: "Ortiz Hung! The County and Town well rid of a worthless vagabond. The man who was so handy with his gun departs this life at the end of a rope."

Constable Nash would live to serve another term as constable before being elected justice of the peace. He died at his home on Fourth Street on December 15, 1905. The old bridge on which Ortiz was lynched was replaced in 1901 by what is known as the Wedding Ring Bridge. Ortiz's lonely apparition is sometimes seen wandering the bridge late at night. Those who've encountered the ghost claim he appears to be confused and angry. His mouth moves to speak but no sound is heard. Then he quickly turns and heads toward the lights of downtown Reno. Can you blame him for being angry?

Downtown Sidewalk

Spots where violence and tragedy have taken place are forever changed. These changes might be imperceptible to most of us. Not so for those who are more sensitive; a psychic can often sense the violence and tragedy that has become imprinted on a location. So it is for a section of sidewalk on North Virginia Street in downtown Reno. It was on this very sidewalk on Thanksgiving Day 1980 that Priscilla Ford committed one of the most horrendous crimes in Nevada history.

It started as just another Thanksgiving in Reno. The weather was mild for November; tourists filled the downtown hotel-casinos in anticipation of a three-day weekend of gaming fun. Hotel kitchens were busy preparing traditional Thanksgiving dinners with all the trimmings. The sidewalks were bustling with people headed toward one casino or the other. Gaming is a 24/7 endeavor; holiday or not, someone is always at work in a casino. During their breaks, casino employees seeking a respite from stale cigarette smoke stepped out for a breath of fresh air. Some ducked in and out of other establishments, wishing friends a happy holiday, perhaps pulling the handles of promising slot machines.

Priscilla Ford was new to Reno, having been in town only two weeks. She was angry and distraught after social services had taken her child from her. She drank nearly half a bottle of wine and devised a plan. She was hearing voices inside her head. And they were telling her to kill. She could not disobey. The fifty-one-year-old got in her blue 1974 Lincoln Continental and slowly drove north on Virginia Street toward downtown.

No one paid any attention to the Lincoln as it passed the Mapes Hotel and crossed First Street. But the voices inside Ford's head were growing louder. Suddenly, she pulled the car onto the sidewalk and floored the gas pedal, plowing through the crowd of people. Oblivious to the scene before her and the agonized cries of her victims and those of horrified onlookers, she drove on. Even as the Lincoln Continental tossed broken and battered bodies into the air, Priscilla Ford continued driving north toward Reno's famous arch. The carnage came to an end when two men pulled their cars in front of the Lincoln at the intersection with Second Street, blocking the car's path.

Only then did Priscilla Ford stop. The destruction she had left behind her was like a scene out of a horror movie. Seven people were dead. Twenty-three others lay injured and maimed on the bloodied sidewalk, which was littered with body parts. A Reno police officer testified at Ford's trial that Ford was heard to say, "The more dead the better. I hope I got seventy-five. A Lincoln Continental can do a lot of damage, can't it?"

Priscilla Ford received the death sentence for her crime. After spending twenty-five years on Nevada's Death Row, she died of natural causes on January 29, 2005, at age seventy-five.

Downtown Reno has changed much in the years since Priscilla Ford shocked the city on Thanksgiving Day 1980. The majority of the hotel-casinos have closed, been demolished, or converted to condominiums and timeshares. Gambling expanded in other states, lessening Reno's popularity. Some would argue that the downtown area is not as lively as it once was. Yet the section of sidewalk on which Ford drove her Lincoln more than thirty years ago appears much the same as it was then. Or does it?

Several people have reported strange feelings of discomfort and nausea while walking along this stretch of sidewalk. One psychic is so overcome by what she calls residual feelings of terror that she won't walk in this area after dark. Then, too, there are the pathetic screams that seem to come from out of nowhere. In one incident, a newlywed husband and wife were walking back to their hotel early one summer morning just before dawn when they were suddenly stopped in their tracks by agonized screams.

"It sounded like someone off in the distance was hurt badly and needing help," the husband later explained. "We called out to them but got no answer. I half expected to see someone lying injured on the sidewalk just up the street from us.

"We followed the screams up the street a few blocks. But we were totally alone. As far as we could see, there was no one on the street but us. I can tell you that the whole thing was a bit unnerving . . . I grabbed my wife's hand and we hurried to our hotel."

Some may say that these feelings are nothing but examples of overworked imaginations. But who is to say whether or not a location is haunted by the sights and sounds of events that once took place there?

University of Nevada, Reno

If you're looking for a place with more than its fair share of ghosts, you might want to consider a school. For some reason, schools seem to have an inordinate amount of spectral residents. The University of Nevada, Reno is no exception. According to one former student, the Church Fine Arts Building is haunted by a long-departed professor. "When I saw him coming toward me in the hall I thought that can't be. This man is a dead ringer for (the professor)," the student reported. "I thought about telling him how much he resembled photographs of the professor then decided against it. We nodded as we passed each other and I turned back to see which way he was going. Wherever he went, it wasn't anywhere in the building. There was no way he could have gotten out of my sight so quickly. Talk about goose bumps. That night I had them."

It is not surprising that most of the ghostly activity takes place in the older buildings and areas of the campus. Frandsen Humanities Building, with its location near Manzanita Lake, is a favorite with photographers. Built in 1917–18 and named in honor of former biology professor Peter Frandsen, the building has some strange quirks. Doors opening and closing on their own, disembodied voices, and misplaced tools and equipment have been reported by maintenance staff working in Frandsen. "It's eerie when you're working alone and hear your name clearly called," one UNR employee told me in an interview. "That has happened to me twice in Frandsen. The first time I thought it was someone outside. When it happened again I wondered if maybe those ghost hunters who came here last year weren't onto something."

The family of Comstock mining millionaire John Mackay felt it was important to give back to their community. As such, the Mackay family presented the Mines Building, and a significant endowment, to the university in honor of John Mackay. Built in 1908 and listed in the National Register of Historic Places in 1982, the building houses the W. M. Keck Museum, the Mackay School of Earth Sciences and Engineering offices, and the DeLaMare Library. Some say the library is haunted by a ghostly presence that delights in turning lights on and off. As if that weren't enough, the playful spirit is also responsible for causing a few of the clocks in the building to stop.

The resident spirit is thought to be that of Katherine Duer Mackay, the beautiful first wife of Clarence Mackay, John Mackay's son. Katherine was a strong-willed woman ahead of her time. A suffragette, she spoke out for women's rights and in 1905 became the first woman to sit on the Roslyn, New York school board. In 1910 Katherine stunned polite upper-crust society when she ran off to Paris with Clarence's surgeon, Dr. Joseph Blake, leaving her husband and three children behind. After divorcing Clarence, Katherine married the doctor in France. There would be no happily ever after for Katherine's second marriage. The union ended in divorce when Blake's roving eye fell on another woman.

A former UNR employee believed that most of the Mackay Building's paranormal activity was centered near a large painting of Katherine in which she is pictured holding a crystal ball of sorts. The larger-than-life-size painting is located in Conference Room 302 and some say it can give a sense of eeriness to anyone who happens to be alone in the room.

Historians look at a haunting tale and try to determine if it's simply the stuff of legend or if there are any historical facts to back it up. The haunting of Lincoln Hall is one such story. Lincoln Hall is one of the oldest buildings on the campus. It was built between 1895 and 1896 to serve as a men's dormitory, and it continues to serve as such today. The stories of a ghostly former resident also continue. And historians will be delighted to know that his existence is based on fact.

On Valentine's Day 1906 the *Nevada State Journal* carried the story of the funeral procession of James Champagne, relating how his fellow University of Nevada, Reno cadets carried his white, flag-draped coffin from the undertaker's building to an awaiting train. The train would travel forty miles south to the tiny town of Genoa where Champagne was to be interred. The article also mentioned the deplorable accident that had taken Champagne's life on February 11. The young man had been alone in his room and cleaning his gun when he accidently shot himself. Some believe he might have intentionally turned the gun on himself. Either way, it is undisputed that James Champagne met an untimely death in Lincoln Hall. He is thought to be the resident ghost that some refer to as Jimmy.

In paranormal circles there are two reasons most often believed to account for a haunting: accidental death and suicide. Suicide is a permanent solution to a temporary problem, unfortunately. If Champagne chose this way to escape his problems, he might regret the decision so much that he refuses to vacate the dormitory. If the young man accidently shot himself, he may also refuse to leave the premises out of anger at the unfairness of his fate.

Not only does the Lincoln Hall spirit make strange noises, an apparition has been seen on occasion by residents of the hall. A former resident of Lincoln Hall told me the following story:

> We all know the story of the ghost around here. When I heard the sobbing one night I thought someone was having fun at my expense, so I ignored it. Then it got so loud I got out of bed and started looking around to see where the noise was coming from. There he was standing in the middle of room. "What on earth?" I asked, still wondering if I weren't being made the butt of someone's joke. "Very funny," I said and reached out to grab whoever it was. There was nothing, only air . . . I'm not sure what it was.

Just another example of the school spirits present at the University of Nevada, Reno.

Hillside Cemetery

Hillside Cemetery in Reno offers a view of the city's brightly lit hotel-casinos and the University of Nevada dorms. Many of Reno's early pioneers rest at the old cemetery, though if developers have their way, this might soon change. Because of its proximity to the University of Nevada, Reno, some would like to see the old cemetery cleared, the bodies disinterred, and new university dorms built on the site. Sadly, the nearly forgotten cemetery has been the victim of careless vandalism and misuse over the years.

While it seems logical that cemeteries may not be the most haunted of places—a cemetery's residents nearly always meet their mortal ends elsewhere—they are not immune from ghosts and hauntings. The person who shared this incident with me worked as a dealer at one of the downtown casinos in 1975. As long as weather permitted he chose to walk to work rather than drive. On this particular afternoon, the temperature soared toward the 100-degree mark as he headed to his job. In a hurry to get to the air-conditioned comfort of the pit, he varied his route and took a shortcut through the Jewish section of the cemetery.

For reasons he can't explain, he felt compelled to glance over his shoulder. Standing a few feet to his left was a tall woman wearing a long black woolen dress; a black hat and veil obscured her face. As he watched her, he couldn't help but wonder why anyone would be out on such a hot day in such heavy clothing.

Trying to decide whether or not to speak to her, he turned away for a split second. When he turned back to comment on the weather, she had vanished. He looked around the headstones and down the paths, but she was nowhere in sight.

He walked through the cemetery many times since that afternoon, but never again saw the mysterious woman in heavy black garb. He does not believe in ghosts, but he is still not convinced that what he saw in the Hillside Cemetery that afternoon wasn't one.

The Woman in Black may not be the only spirit at Hillside; the cemetery is unique in that someone actually did die on the grounds. No sightings have been reported of this man's ghost, but the story of his tragic death has become part of Reno lore.

World War I was raging across Europe when nineteen-year-old William Blanchfield entered the Royal Flying Corps of Great Britain.

A fearless pilot, Blanchfield honed his skills while taking part in several decisive air battles.

When the war ended, Blanchfield immigrated to the United States and applied for citizenship. The twenty-six-year-old aviator went to work for the U.S. Postal Service as an airmail pilot in 1921. His assigned route was the Reno to Elko run. Every morning at 7:50 the intrepid young pilot flew out of Reno in a refitted World War I–era de Havilland. He would land in Elko two and a half hours later. Like the previous century's Pony Express riders, the airmail pilots captured the public's imagination. Blanchfield's exploits as an aviator were legendary among Renoites, who eagerly read about his adventures. The handsome Irishman racked up 709 hours and nearly sixty-three thousand miles flying across the Nevada desert. When faced with raging winds and sub-zero temperatures that forced him to land in remote areas, he did so with aplomb. Once during a blinding snowstorm his plane crashed into deep snow. Knocked unconscious, Blanchfield woke to find himself trapped. He struggled with his seatbelts and eventually pulled himself from the wreckage.

Mindful of his duty as a mail carrier, he dragged the heavy sacks of mail from the plane and carried them to the railroad tracks. There, he waited in the snow for hours until he could flag down the train. A remarkable feat, he made sure the mail arrived in Elko in time for another plane to fly it on to Salt Lake.

In a strange way, Blanchfield's death was just as remarkable. It began with the untimely death of his dear friend Samuel Gerrans, a mechanic at the Reno airfield. The men had been friends since flying together in the war, and news of Gerrans's death hit Blanchfield hard.

Blanchfield formulated a plan while he waited for the train bearing Gerrans's body to arrive in Reno. He would seek permission to do three flybys over his friend's graveside ceremony at Hillside Cemetery. On the last flyby he would drop a wreath onto the grave. It seemed like a good idea to the Postal Service superintendent, who granted the young aviator's request.

On August 1, 1924, friends and relatives gathered at Samuel Gerrans's graveside in the Knights of Pythias section of Hillside Cemetery. Sunlight streamed down from the cloudless blue sky. Reverend

Brewster Adams cleared his throat, ready to conclude the service. Blanchfield's de Havilland biplane soared over the grave and then circled around for a second pass. As it came in, the plane was less than five hundred feet above the mourners, who could clearly see William Blanchfield sitting in the open cockpit. In his hand was the wreath he was about to drop over his friend's flag-draped coffin. The biplane then turned south for the third and final pass.

"For inasmuch hath it pleased Almighty God in his infinite wisdom to take out of this world the soul of our beloved brother, we therefore commit his body to the grave. Earth unto earth, dust unto dust, ashes unto ashes," Reverend Adams said.

The mourners, their eyes turned skyward, gasped as a sudden gust of wind tossed Blanchfield's plane like it was a scrap of paper fluttering in the breeze. The plane nosedived into a tangle of telephone wires and slid into the side of a nearby house. The gas tank exploded with a thunderous roar, sending flames shooting in all directions. The house was destroyed, although its occupants were able to escape unharmed. Witnesses watching from a few yards away claimed to have heard "a blood-curdling scream" at the instant of impact.

People stared in stunned disbelief. Women fainted in horror. Men rushed to the site to aid their friend and colleague. On seeing the charred and twisted wreckage, one of the men commented sadly, "William Blanchfield has gone west."

Reno was shocked. Throughout the city, people spoke of the aviator in reverent tones. Blanchfield, known affectionately as "Big Bill," had been a hero to so many people, especially the youngsters who hoped someday to emulate his airborne feats.

Later, F. E. Caldwell, manager of the airfield where Gerrans and Blanchfield worked, would say, "Blanchfield has held the esteem and affection of the entire air mail service from the east coast to the west. One of the most brilliant fliers in the service, he won the highest admiration from everyone with whom he came in contact."

William F. Blanchfield's funeral was held at St. Thomas Aquinas Church in Reno. He was buried with full military honors in Mountain View Cemetery on August 4, 1924. The Reno Air Field was renamed in his honor.

A week after the aviator's death, the superintendent who had given his permission to use the airmail service plane for the flyby at Gerrans's funeral was asked to resign. Such use of a service plane was contrary to regulations.

Shortly before St. Patrick's Day 1925 a small package from County Cork Ireland arrived at the office of the manager of the cemetery. Inside were a small mound of shamrocks and a note from William Blanchfield's mother, asking that they be placed on her son's grave on Ireland's special day. Mrs. Blanchfield continued to send shamrocks to adorn her son's grave on St. Patrick's Day every year until her death.

Washoe County Courthouse

The Washoe County Courthouse in downtown Reno was made famous by the early-twentieth-century screen stars who once appeared within its confines seeking a Nevada-style quickie divorce. This was in an era before divorce was quick and commonplace across the country. At the time Reno was known as the country's divorce capital, despite the fact that there were always more marriage licenses than divorce decrees obtained at the Washoe County Courthouse. Reno earned its reputation by becoming the hotspot for Hollywood elite who wanted to get out of unhappy marriages. Some of the biggest names in showbiz came through the doors of the courthouse.

The courthouse steps were featured in scenes of Marilyn Monroe's last film, *The Misfits*. Monroe was filmed standing at the courthouse door in a scene with Kevin McCarthy, who played her husband. A long-held Reno rumor maintains that Monroe kissed one of the courthouse pillars in the film. If she did do so, the scene ended up on the cutting-room floor. Some of the fans who stood in the hot sun and watched the filming back in 1960 say she did. Others say she did not. Either way, kissing a pillar after obtaining a divorce was considered good luck for the person doing the kissing.

Built in 1911, the Washoe County Courthouse was designed by Frederick DeLongchamps, one of Reno's preeminent architects. The building is said to be haunted by a few ghosts. One is that of an elderly judge who stepped out from his chambers for a smoke.

Apparently, his honor missed his footing and fell down the stairs, breaking his neck.

Upstairs in the courthouse's top floor is the old jail that is no longer in use. However, some of those who've worked up there on the late shift claim that some mighty strange things occur. The heavy iron jail doors have been known to slam open and shut. One guard said, "Just when you think you are the only person on the floor the doors will clang open and the sound of shuffling feet will echo through the jail."

Some believe J.W. Rover has returned from the grave to proclaim his innocence once again. Rover was hanged in the courtyard of the old brick courthouse, in the approximate area where the marriage license division is today.

Rover met his end February 19, 1878, a day that brought an icy rain sweeping across Reno. During the morning a light snow began to fall. J.W. Rover was set to die that day for the gruesome murder of L.N. Sharp out in the Black Rock Desert north of the city. In a final effort to save their client's skin, Rover's attorneys called for a special sheriff's jury to determine his sanity. If he were judged insane he could live out his days in prison, a far more inviting prospect than that offered by the gallows.

Rover stood trial twice. Both times his case went all the way to the Nevada Supreme Court. A glimmer of hope had sustained the condemned man in the months preceding his final trial. With his options having run out, Rover nervously paced the tiny cell and prayed for a miracle.

A crowd gathered in the county courthouse, wondering if Rover would hang. At 8:00, the jury filed into the courthouse. Agreement meant that Rover was insane and couldn't be hanged. After four hours of deliberation, the announcement was made: the jury could not reach an agreement. Thus the fate of J.W. Rover was settled.

The forty-eight-year-old New York native would hang, leaving behind a wife and three children in San Joaquin County, California. Sheriff James Kinkead saw no reason to delay the inevitable. He and Sheriff Lamb were ready to escort Rover to his execution. Weeping bitterly, Rover stood and then nearly collapsed. Two priests assisted him as he shuffled toward his doom. They would stay on the scaffold and pray with him until the very end. Rover slowly walked up the gallows steps and seated himself in the only available chair. This execution was not to be public. It would take place in the courtyard, hidden from public view by a tall fence.

Protocol required Sheriff Kinkead to invite two hundred men to witness the proceedings. Hundreds more attempted to catch a glimpse over the fence surrounding the courtyard. Witnesses shivered in the cold. Snow lay in drifts and continued to fall. Rover was asked if he had any final words. He nodded silently, and then stood and cleared his throat: "Gentlemen—I have nothing much to say; I am so prostrated by this long persecution, that I am unable to say what I desire to, and the time too, will not admit of it."

Somehow he found the time. Rover addressed the crowd for another fifty-two minutes, claiming his conviction was a conspiracy between the state's attorney and his accuser, one Mr. McWorthy, who Rover claimed was the actual murderer. His final words spoken, J.W. Rover sat down and gazed out at the shivering crowd. Wind blew the snow in all directions. Men shifted their weight from foot to foot trying to keep warm. Anxious to get back to the comfort of a hot stove, the two sheriffs quickly bound Rover's hands and led him to the awaiting rope. Sheriff Lamb placed the rope around his neck and Sheriff Kinkead placed the black hood over his head.

"Oh! Lamb," Rover said softly.

The *Daily Nevada State Journal* of February 20, 1878, described the scene as such: "The signal was given, and the trap sprung. Rover has gone, and with his death the law is satisfied. Let us all think as charitably as possible of the deceased, who has gone where none but his God can judge him."

Then, as now, death doesn't necessarily decrease one's newsworthiness. Belief in Rover's innocence continued long after his execution. Within a week of the hanging, the *Reno Gazette* printed the following story.

Rover Visits Mrs. Bowers
Mrs. Bowers, the Washoe seeress called on Gen. Clark the other day and said to him, "General, Rover was innocent."
"How do you know?" said he.
She answered. "I was eating dinner when someone tapped me on the shoulder and I heard a voice say, 'I am J. W. Rover, and have just been hanged in Reno, but I am innocent.'" Until this visit

Mrs. Bowers declares that she did not know that Rover had been hanged. Since this occurrence the Carson spiritualists have held three or four séances; Rover is called for, appears and tells the same old story, so oft repeated.

Twenty years passed and the question of Rover's guilt still loomed for some. Then the following story appeared in the July 24, 1899 issue of the *Reno Gazette*:

Slightly Mistaken

The Carson News says that McWorthy, the rabbit hole sulphur man, who early in the 70's was the principle [*sic*] prosecuting witness in the trial of J. W. Rover for the murder of I. N. Sharp at Rabbit Hole, Humboldt County, died in Arizona a few years ago and confessed to being the murderer of Sharp, who Rover was hung for killing, in the Court House yard of Washoe County. The News is mistaken, for McWorthy is alive today and living in Oakland. Rover killed sharp and paid the penalty with his own life.

Interestingly enough, there is no mention of McWorthy's outrageous indignation at having been labeled a murderer, or how the *Reno Gazette* came to know his whereabouts. If the claims were true and Rover was indeed innocent, it would be easy to understand why he still haunts the courthouse.

Olivia Miller's Unsuccessful Escape

Another of the courthouse area's alleged ghosts, that of Olivia Miller, has been spotted numerous times. The *Weekly Nevada State Journal* of September 2, 1876 reported on Miller's death and burial: "At the altar of sin she sacrificed everything. She sleeps 'unwept, unhonored, and unsung.' Let her fate be a warning. Truly, 'the wages of sin is death.'"

Miller's ordeal began on the morning of July 16, 1876, when Reno undertaker W. Sanders took his horse and buggy nine miles north to the Junction House in Poeville. He and Sheriff Jones had come to pick up the body of Samuel Miller, Olivia Miller's husband, and take it back to Reno for proper burial. What they found stunned them.

Miller's body lay face down in the dirt. His head had been bashed in with an axe wielded by handyman George DeLong. While Olivia Miller wrung her hands and wept at the sight of her dead husband, DeLong calmly told the story of Miller's demise, claiming self defense. Samuel Miller was a heavy drinker. On the night of his death he had come home drunk and angry. When DeLong refused to do a small task for him, Miller became enraged and threatened him with a rope. Between sobs, Mrs. Miller corroborated the story.

Sheriff Jones was suspicious. The furtive looks that passed between Mrs. Miller and DeLong had not escaped his notice; neither had their whispering to each other when they thought no one was watching. Maybe Miller had come home unexpectedly and caught the two of them together. But that seemed unlikely.

DeLong was young and handsome. His piercing dark eyes, coal-black hair, and luxuriant mustache would surely catch the eye of any young woman. Watching Olivia as she stumbled around in feigned grief, the sheriff could see nothing comely about old Mrs. Miller. She was at least forty, and stout for a woman. Her face was jowly and flushed like someone who drank too much liquor. If DeLong had killed for her, the sheriff reasoned, he must be half blind and out of his mind. Regardless, the sheriff was sure that the two of them had some scheme going.

He had no doubt that the pair was lying about how Mr. Miller had met his death. There was nothing to do but arrest DeLong for murder and Olivia Miller as his accomplice.

DeLong was promptly taken to the Reno jail while the sheriff searched for a more suitable place to keep his female prisoner overnight. The jail was no place for a woman, even one as mean as Olivia Miller, to be after dark. It was decided that she would spend her nights in the district attorney's offices. But being locked up didn't suit the widow Miller. She waited until well after midnight, and then she pried the lock off the door and promptly escaped to a friend's ranch. There she stayed until the sheriff caught up with her and the friend who had harbored her. Back to the district attorney's office she went.

A week passed; the searing heat of August swept across the Truckee Meadows on dry winds. Mrs. Miller grew restless in the district attorney's cramped office. She yearned to look up and see the sky overhead, to feel the sunshine on her face, to be free in the wide-open space of the desert. She was determined to escape. This time she would not bother with the lock on the door; a guard had boasted to her that it was double bolted and escape proof. Still, she was determined to be free one way or the other. She sat in the darkness and listened as the clock ticked off the hours. It was a few minutes after four on September 2, 1876, when she jumped up and sprang into action.

Raising the window to allow for her girth, Mrs. Miller gazed a moment at the courtyard twenty feet below. It wasn't that far down, she reasoned; she could do it. She climbed onto the sill and jumped. She died on impact, thus solving the problem of how best to incarcerate a woman. Her accomplice, George DeLong, was eventually convicted of manslaughter, but the handsome young man was spared the hangman's noose. He spent the next nine years at the state prison in Carson City.

Be alert when walking along the Reno Riverwalk near the back of the courthouse. The ghostly Mrs. Olivia Miller, described as a heavyset blonde woman, is known to favor this area. She means no harm, but she is confused. What went wrong with her perfect escape plan?

Where is Roy Frisch?

Unexplained disappearances are always unsettling, and such mysteries often capture the public's imagination. One of the most enduring mysteries in Reno concerns the disappearance of Roy Frisch.

The evening of March 22, 1934, started off in a flurry of activity in the Frisch household. A bridge party was planned for that night at the Frisch home, and Mrs. Frisch and her daughters had spent the day preparing for the evening's activities. Neither a fan of cards nor of the noisy banter that accompanied his mother's bridge parties, Roy Frisch decided to see *Gallant Lady*, the new movie showing at the Majestic Theater, rather than suffer through the party.

"I'm going to a show. I'll be home early." With those words, Roy Frisch walked out the front door of the home he shared with his widowed mother and two sisters on the corner of Court and

Belmont (now Arlington) Streets. His family watched him close the door, never guessing it would be the last time they ever saw him.

Frisch had a long day ahead of him. He was scheduled to leave for New York early the next morning. The bank employee's testimony in a federal fraud case had already resulted in four convictions and now he was under subpoena to testify in court against his former employers, Reno underworld figures James McKay and Bill Graham. A quiet man, any apprehension Frisch may have felt concerning his appearance in federal court was kept from those closest to him.

He stepped onto the sidewalk at 7:45 P.M. Light rain had fallen across the Truckee Meadows, filling the air with the aroma of sagebrush and pine. Low clouds obscured the crescent moon and prevented the temperature from dropping. It was a perfect spring night in Reno, so Frisch left his car parked in the garage. He decided to walk to the Majestic Theater on the corner of West First and Center Streets, several blocks away. Stopping just long enough to adjust his gray fedora, he glanced briefly back at his home before turning and heading east on Court Street.

At forty-five, Frisch was one of the city's upstanding citizens. His father, Charles Jacob, had come from Switzerland as a teenager to work on the Comstock; he later settled in Reno and operated the Pyramid House on the corner of Commercial Row and Lake Street. Dead seven years, the elder Frisch would have been proud of Roy for accepting the responsibility of testifying against McKay and Graham. As a cashier at the Riverside Bank, Roy had inadvertently found himself working for the two crime bosses. On occasion, he had even pointed out to them that some of their bank transactions were questionable. His testimony, prosecutors believed, would provide the evidence necessary to secure a conviction. Frisch would testify and do what was right. He always had; he had fought in World War I and served as both a Reno city councilman and the county assessor.

Once at the theater, Frisch chose a seat in the loge. An usher later remembered seeing him there, apparently engrossed in the film. After the movie Frisch and a friend walked down Virginia Street together. At Court Street they went their separate ways, with Roy walking west along Court. Halfway between his home and the sheriff's office, he encountered another friend. According to that man, it was 10:15 when they stopped to chat. The conversation was brief. They said their goodbyes and parted company. It was the last time anyone other than his killer would see Roy Frisch.

The bridge party ended shortly before 2 A.M. The guests gone and the tables cleared, Mrs. Frisch looked in at her son's bedroom at half past two. The coverlet on his bed was still neat and unturned. Before she retired for the evening, Mrs. Frisch turned the porch light on for Roy. The light was still shining when she woke the next morning.

Because Frisch was under federal subpoena his disappearance was viewed with suspicion from the start. Friends and relatives were contacted. No one knew where he was. As the day wore on with no sign of her son, Mrs. Frisch's motherly concern turned to fear. Where was her oldest child?

A description of the missing man was teletyped across the country. Two days passed with no word on Frisch's whereabouts. The search intensified when Sheriff Russell Trathen announced that he would call in 120 Nevada National Guardsmen to help search for the missing man. Everyone had a theory as to Frisch's fate; some posited that he was a victim of amnesia, or that he had been kidnapped for ransom. The most popular theory was that Frisch had been abducted and, in the parlance of the day, "taken for a ride" in retaliation for his earlier testimony, which had helped send four men to prison for defrauding an elderly hotelkeeper out of his $140,000 life savings. It was also noted that without Frisch's testimony the government's case against McKay and Graham was severely weakened.

Three days after Frisch's disappearance, Reno police chief J. M. Kirkley asked federal investigators to help in the case. The Washoe County commissioners unanimously approved a resolution that authorized the sheriff to offer rewards totaling $1,000 for information on Frisch's whereabouts. Acting Governor Morley Griswold added his concerns for solving the case with a statement that read, in part, "I will use all of the resources of the state of Nevada to apprehend and to bring to justice anyone who may be responsible for the disappearance of, or to find, an esteemed citizen who has disappeared.

"Full instructions have been given for a full and thorough investigation to ascertain the true facts."

Searchers combed through the sagebrush around Peavine Mountain and in the abandoned cabins along the Truckee River. Grappling hooks were used to drag the river bottom. Days slipped into weeks with no sign of Roy Frisch.

Two months after Frisch's disappearance, a revised indictment was issued in the United States District Court against James McKay and William Graham. They were charged with three, instead of the original two, counts of mail fraud. They pled not guilty and were freed on $10,000 bail each.

The mail fraud trial of McKay and Graham proceeded in July as scheduled. Taking Frisch's place as a principal witness was J. M Fuetsch, a former coworker in the now-defunct Riverside Bank. On the witness stand, Fuetsch said of Frisch: "He told me he would rather be dead than get mixed up in this thing. But on the night he disappeared he seemed to be in the best spirits I ever saw him. He had talked with me about what he intended to do the next day and seemed to have no intention of committing suicide or disappearing . . . It is my opinion that he was taken for a ride."

It was an opinion shared by more than just Fuetsch. A year after Roy Frisch went missing, two Renoites stood trial in San Francisco federal court for conspiring to harbor fugitive Lester Gillis, aka "Baby Face" Nelson, while he resided in Reno. The two people involved knew Nelson as "Jimmy Burnell" and claimed to have no knowledge of the gangster's true identity, though they did realize he had a volatile temper. During questioning, they revealed a potential connection between Nelson and one of the men Roy Frisch was to testify against.

The prosecutor asked the men, "Was the person you knew as Jimmy Burnell a chauffeur to William Graham?"

"Yes, he was," the defendants answered.

Later, John Paul Chase, an Alcatraz inmate and Nelson associate serving time for the November 1934 murder of two FBI agents during the shootout that had also claimed Nelson's life, claimed to have seen Roy Frisch murdered by Baby Face Nelson. According to Chase, he and Nelson came to Reno on March 20, 1934. On the night of March 22 they were driving through town when they happened upon Frisch. Nelson jumped out of the car, knocked him out with the butt of his gun, and dragged him into the car.

They then drove to a Reno garage where the unconscious Frisch was transferred to another car and shot in the head. His body was then driven some 150 miles from Reno and dumped down an abandoned mine shaft. Authorities believed this location was probably somewhere around Hawthorne, where the Nelson gang was known to have hidden out. A search of the area turned up nothing.

By 1938, Roy Frisch had been gone four years. After two trials and two deadlocked juries, the government proceeded with its third mail fraud case against James McKay and William Graham. On February 12, 1939, James McKay and William Graham were found guilty of mail fraud and of operating a swindling ring. They were each ordered to pay $11,000 in fines and sentenced to serve nine years in Leavenworth Federal Penitentiary.

Seven years after her son's disappearance, Mrs. Frisch petitioned the district court to have him legally declared dead. The order was entered by Judge Curler on July 15, 1941.

McKay and Graham were paroled in October 1945 and returned to Reno after having served six years of their sentences. In 1950 the two men were given full pardons by President Harry S. Truman, thanks in part to lobbying by Nevada senator Pat McCarran, whose Reno home was, incidentally, located across the street from the Frisch family home.

The Frisch family still owns the home on the corner of Court and Arlington Streets. It has been converted to attorneys' offices and other businesses. The light is still left on every night for Roy. Some who've worked within the building claim it is haunted by a male presence. Heavy footsteps and a booming cough have been reported. So too have cold spots. Perhaps Roy has returned home after all.

Cal Neva Resort

The Cal Neva Resort is located on the shores of Lake Tahoe's Crystal Bay amid tall pine trees and enormous granite boulders. Breathtaking views of the lake can be had from anywhere on the property. This is one reason film stars regularly stayed here in the 1950s and

1960s. It's rumored that Frank Sinatra came here in the early 1950s to get over the end of his marriage to Hollywood beauty Ava Gardner. He fell in love with the area and decided to purchase the Cal Neva in 1960. It was the perfect spot to entertain friends, and Rat Pack members Peter Lawford, Joey Bishop, Sammy Davis Jr., and Dean Martin all came to the Cal Neva. So did Marilyn Monroe.

A week before her 1962 death, Marilyn came to the Cal Neva hoping to find peace. Her life was a train wreck. She was a star whose dazzle was fading fast. Notorious for being late to the set, she had been fired from her latest film, *Something's Got to Give*, and her ego was bruised. Her marriage to Arthur Miller was over and so were her relationships with the Kennedy brothers, John F. and Robert.

According to some, these last days of her life were spent in a drug-induced stupor, with Marilyn alone and forgotten in the cabin Frank had assigned to her. Was she tormented to the point of madness? Ghost investigators the world over have come to Cabin 3 at the Cal Neva to pay homage to Monroe and to attempt contact with her spirit. She is still here, some say. EVP (electronic voice phenomena) has been recorded in the cabin. One voice was very clearly that of a young woman's breathy response to the question of whether or not she was happy now. The answer was yes.

A ghostly Marilyn Monroe has also been seen strutting across the Cal Neva's parking lot late at night. In one incident that took place on a snowy autumn night, a security guard was called to a certain floor of the new tower. Someone was loudly crying in the hallway. He stepped in the elevator and smiled to himself, believing the disturbance was probably a lovers' quarrel and that the parties would have kissed and made up by the time he got there. But that wasn't the case. The guard stepped out of the elevator and encountered a young blonde in a form-fitting red dress, looking like Marilyn Monroe.

"Do you need help, miss?" he asked.

She stared blankly at him, as if she didn't understand him.

"What's your name?"

His breath caught in his throat as she calmly turned from him and walked straight through the wall. From then on he was certain he had spoken to the ghost of Marilyn Monroe.

If Marilyn is indeed haunting the property, she is not alone in doing so. Many believe that Frank Sinatra, whose ownership of the resort came to a bitter and inglorious end, is still here in spirit.

With Sinatra in charge, the Cal Neva prospered. The lodge's popularity soared, and some believed that Sinatra had plans to expand his hospitality business by opening a fabulous nightclub in Reno. The truth was, barely a year after Marilyn's death, Frank Sinatra's ownership of the Cal Neva was rapidly coming to an end.

The Nevada Gaming Commission implemented its "Black Book" of excluded persons in 1960. The report listed those individuals— most of them involved in organized crime—who were banned from all of the state's gaming facilities. Chicago mob boss Sam Giancana was on the original list of eleven names. If Frank Sinatra was aware of this fact, he chose to ignore it.

In July 1963 Sam Giancana was seeing Phyllis McGuire, a member of the popular singing group the McGuire Sisters. Sinatra's trouble started when the McGuire Sisters arrived at the Cal Neva for their appearance in the resort's showroom. Giancana was besotted with Phyllis and decided to visit her there. According to some sources, Sinatra not only gave Giancana access to the Cal Neva, but also allowed him to stay in one of the cabins. When this fact came to light the Nevada Gaming Commission was not amused.

On August 29, 1963, Edward A. Olsen, chairman of the Gaming Commission, received a phone call from a Sinatra employee who informed him that Sinatra was upset at publicity surrounding the commission's investigation into Giancana's presence at the Cal Neva. Apparently word had leaked to the media concerning their investigation of the Cal Neva's direct violation of gaming commission rules; like it or not, Sinatra had some explaining to do.

Two days later a furious Frank Sinatra called Olsen himself. The first thing he wanted to know was why Olsen wouldn't come to the Cal Neva and meet with him in person. When he was told that wasn't going to happen, Sinatra cursed at Olsen. Throughout the conversation, Sinatra's speech was punctuated by a barrage of four-letter words. Sinatra continued to demand that Olsen travel to the Cal Neva to meet with him.

Olsen refused. Accustomed to getting his own way, Sinatra ranted and raved, and then attempted to ride out the controversy.

But his celebrity status did little to deter the commission's prosecution of the case. For his blatant disregard of the gaming commission's regulations, Frank Sinatra's license was revoked after a hearing. Even Sinatra's friends in high places, such as President Kennedy, couldn't help him. While riding in a parade with Nevada governor Grant Sawyer, Kennedy asked, "Aren't you people being a little hard on Frank out here?" Sawyer didn't reply, and the revocation stood. Not only was Sinatra forced to give up ownership of the Cal Neva, but he was also forced to relinquish the shares he owned in the Sands in Las Vegas as well.

More than fifty years have passed since Frank Sinatra owned the Cal Neva, but he is not forgotten here. The showroom bears his name, photos of him line the hallway outside the showroom, and his piano is displayed center stage. It's not surprising that the showroom and the backstage area are most often associated with Sinatra sightings or hauntings.

Mobster Sam Giancana reportedly sat backstage, hidden from view as he watched Phyllis McGuire perform. During an investigation of the area a sensitive felt the presence of someone who "hadn't been very nice in life . . . Someone a little rough around the edges." Those involved in the investigation believed this might have been either Sam Giancana or one of his bodyguards.

Shortly after the arrival of Frank Sinatra's piano, a strange incident occurred: a large photo of the singer in his prime that had stood on the stage mysteriously vanished, and it has never been found. The ghostly Sinatra is also said to be responsible for the late-night piano music that is sometimes heard coming from the darkened showroom.

Many Cal Neva employees tell of ghostly encounters with the singer they reverently refer to as "Frank." One person told of seeing a tall figure he believed was Frank sauntering across the stage. "Like he was singing or entertaining an audience," the witness explained.

A young woman who has been brushed against by an unseen presence in the showroom several times knows it was the spirit of Frank Sinatra. "He's returned here because he loved this place so much!" the woman told me in an interview. The woman, born long after Sinatra lost ownership of the resort, added, "And no one can kick him out of here this time around!"

Occasionally the sound of laughter drifts through the empty showroom. Equipment has been known to quit working for no apparent reason, especially if someone had the audacity to question the ghost stories. Don't doubt the presence of Frank. To do so may bring more than the doubter bargained for, according to some employees. During a late-afternoon rehearsal, a member of the group that was performing in the showroom decided to make light of the ghosts of Frank and Marilyn.

No sooner had he announced that ghostly sightings were just products of overworked imaginations than all of the equipment stopped working. After an hour of trying to find the source of the problem, everyone gave up; there was nothing more for them to do but leave the stage. It was the last time they joked about the ghosts at the Cal Neva.

Some employees say the showroom light booth is also the site of ghostly activity. A long-dead lighting technician is thought to be responsible for items being moved or misplaced in the booth. Only a few employees have the key to the light booth, which is always locked. A person told of returning to the light booth and finding lights he'd turned off the night before turned on and shining brightly in the morning. Another said she had watched one night as a heavy door in the light booth that can barely be pushed open with both hands slowly opened of its own volition. While she was trying to figure out how the door had opened, it closed with a bang.

Those who've performed in the showroom say that it is acoustically superb, exactly what Frank Sinatra wanted. This could be reason his spirit is said to still be on the premises.

Thunderbird Lodge

It was springtime. The sun shone brightly in a clear blue sky, but it was still cold enough that scattered patches of snow covered the ground. Three vehicles pulled into the narrow driveway of the stately Thunderbird Lodge, located on the northeast shore of Lake Tahoe. They held a reality-television film crew who was there to determine just who, or what, might be haunting the grounds of the Thunderbird. They were accompanied by a psychic who had previously made contact with those on the other side, as well as her skeptical sidekick. Both had previously visited the lodge.

The psychic slid from the backseat of one of the black SUVs. She glanced out at Lake Tahoe, and then on very high heels hurried into the warmth of the main building. A photograph of George Whittell caught her eye as she walked through the lodge. She stopped and concentrated on it a moment. "Not a very nice man," she said. "I don't like him."

Hours later, during filming in the boathouse, she would be attacked by an unseen force that pulled her hair. The memory of what she said earlier about George Whittell came rushing back to those who had witnessed it. Whittell, the not very nice man, was perhaps still in residence at his Thunderbird Lodge. Never much of a humanitarian, the ghostly Whittell might resent the intrusion of ghost hunters into his private residence. Others believe the boathouse is haunted by angry Native American spirits who are displeased with how their beautiful lake and land have been misused.

The next stop for the film crew was a room that had been sealed up a number of years earlier. Standing at the door's edge, the crew heard to the sound of dripping water. This is where George Whittell wanted his indoor pool. While working in this room during the pool's construction, a workman fell from a ladder to his death. After the unfortunate man's body was removed, Whittell ordered that everything be left as it was and that the room be sealed up. Perhaps it was superstition that drove him to this decision, or just another example of his eccentricity.

Most of those who enjoy a good haunting tale are familiar with the Winchester Mansion in San Jose, California, where the reclusive and eccentric Sarah Winchester spent some of her neverending supply of cash on a lavish and most unusual home for herself. Few have heard of Nevada's George Whittell, an eccentric millionaire with money to burn and a desire for seclusion.

Like Sarah Winchester, George Whittell inherited more money than he could spend in several lifetimes. "The Captain," as he liked to be called, would never work a day in his life, nor would he ever worry over finances. In a time when the rest of the nation was suffering through the horror of the Great Depression, Whittell had millions to do with as he chose. He indulged himself with the latest technology, including fast cars, planes, and boats.

By 1936 he owned more than forty thousand acres and twenty-seven miles of Lake Tahoe's pristine Eastern Shore. And like other wealthy San Franciscans, he wanted a summer home at the lake. To that end he commissioned top Nevada architect Frederic J. DeLongchamps to design a summer cottage on his vast lakefront acreage. A "cottage" to Whittell and his ilk was vastly different from what most consider a cottage. This would not be some rustic hunting shack. All buildings were to blend aesthetically with their surroundings and none should detract from the beauty of the lake. Using European master craftsmen and ironworkers, as well as local stonemasons, DeLongchamps brought Whittell's dream to fruition. Situated at the water's edge, the completed lodge was everything George Whittell had dreamed it would be, easily the most fabulous residence on the lake.

Here George Whittell entertained showbiz notables, sports figures, scoundrels, showgirls, and politicians. Eventually rumors flew around the lake about the wild parties and other outrageous goings-on at the Whittell Estate. While his wife spent most of her time in Paris, Whittell played host to a bevy of young ladies. It was whispered that showgirls from nearby hotel-casinos regularly strutted their stuff in the card house at the Whittell Estate. The site of several high-stakes card games and late-night parties, the card house was connected to the main house by six-hundred-foot tunnel that also led to the boathouse. It was one of George Whittell's favorite areas at the lodge.

Whittell kept exotic animals at his estate, and was rumored to permit all of them, including his pet lion Bill, free reign of the grounds. This provided just another reason for the dislike his neighbors had for the eccentric Whittell. He returned the favor. According to some stories he went out of his way to make himself a nuisance to them. When he wanted a boat in 1939, he hired a naval architect to design a yacht. The resulting fifty-five-foot craft was christened *Thunderbird* and built of Honduran mahogany hardwoods, stainless steel, and crystal at a cost of $87,000. While racing his sleek *Thunderbird* around the lake, Whittell made as much noise as he could. And if that wasn't enough, he kept his record player at full volume well into the night.

Whittell also drew up plans for developing some of his extensive acreage at Incline on the North Shore of the lake. For some reason he decided against the idea of building hotel-casinos and resorts. Had he done so this area of the lake would be very different than it is today. Whether his decision was made with an eye toward preservation or simply as a means of keeping people and intrusion at bay, it has proven fortuitous for future generations who can continue to enjoy the shoreline's pristine beauty.

Certainly there is no place in Nevada quite like George Whittell's former home, now known as the Thunderbird Lodge at Incline Village. Located two miles south of Sand Harbor, the picturesque lodge is overseen by the non-profit Thunderbird Lodge Preservation Society, which offers tours to the public from spring to late fall. It is a must-see for history buffs, those who appreciate fine architecture and natural beauty, and of course, ghost hunters. Some ghostly activity has been reported in the former cook and butler's home (now the gift shop), but most of the paranormal activity seems to take place in the boathouse and the old pool house. Because the Thunderbird Lodge sits on ground where the Washoe once lived, some believe there is a large amount of Native American spirit activity in the boathouse. Chanting and rhythmic drum beatings are two unexplained sounds that were clearly heard when only two people were present in the boathouse. Some of these sounds were recorded as EVP as well.

Because he loved his Thunderbird Lodge, it is easy to see why George Whittell himself may well be haunting his former home.

Carson City and the Carson Valley

CHRISTOPHER "KIT" CARSON SERVED AS A SCOUT FOR JOHN C. Fremont's 1842–1845 expedition of the West. Carson's abilities as a scout so impressed Fremont that he named the Carson River for him in recognition of his outstanding service. Nevada's state capital was later named in honor of him, even though he never actually set foot in the city that bears his name.

When Mormon pioneers were dispatched to settle this far-flung area of Utah Territory, they called it Carson County. In 1855 Orson Hyde was appointed probate judge to oversee the new county. During his time in Carson County, Hyde built a sawmill in Franktown in the Washoe Valley and surveyed the town of Mormon Station, which he renamed Genoa. Some believe that Hyde, along with a number of other characters from the region's colorful and sometimes violent history, still has a presence here.

The Haunted Hanging Tree and Adam Uber's Curse

Are curses effective? That depends on who you ask. Some may tell you that curses are nothing but silly superstition. Those in the Carson Valley may disagree. Curses are a popular part of the Carson

Valley's interesting history, and none has a story more tragic than that of Adam Uber, a friendless young man who became the victim of a mob on a cold November night in 1897. No one in Genoa liked Adam Uber. Consequently, no one came to his defense that night.

It all started in a Gardnerville bar. When Hans Anderson saw Uber alone at the bar, he sauntered up to him and loudly announced his intent to beat him silly. He finished his threat by slapping Uber's back—a fatal mistake. Uber pulled his gun and shot his tormentor.

Anderson died on the barroom floor and Uber was taken to the Genoa jail. In killing a town favorite, he had incurred the town's wrath and sealed his own fate.

Emboldened by alcohol, a group of men met and decided that Uber should pay for his crime without the benefit of a trial. As Uber cowered in his cell, the angry mob cut the phone lines and rushed the jail. The sheriff and a constable were held at gunpoint while Uber was pulled from his cell and dragged outside toward a group of cottonwood trees.

As the mob yanked him up and knotted the noose around his neck, Adam Uber cursed each one of them and said that his curse would follow through for seven generations. Someone yanked the rope and Uber was hoisted into eternity. Not satisfied with their cruel deed, some of the crowd pulled their guns and shot wildly at Uber's lifeless body as it swung in the tree.

The lynching shocked many in the state. The *Carson Appeal* stated the lynching was as needless as it was cowardly. There was no possible excuse for the action and it was attended by circumstances of extreme cruelty and brutality.

Appalled by the senseless act, Governor Reinhold Sadler offered a $500 reward for the arrest and conviction of those responsible. Genoa kept its sordid secret. No arrests were made and the reward was never collected.

This wasn't the last of Adam Uber. One by one, his angry ghost visited those who had ridden with the lynching party that night. As any ghost researcher knows, a vengeful ghost is the worst sort. Those who'd been involved in Uber's murder cringed in fear lest the ghost should come to see them. A few of those who'd help to string up Uber died by their own hands, and one of the men was maimed in a freak runaway-horse accident very near the spot where

Uber met his gruesome fate. All involved met terrible ends. Sadly, some of their family members also suffered.

The tall group of cottonwood trees where Adam Uber was hanged still stands along Genoa Lane. The phantom of Adam Uber can be seen hovering nearby on certain moonlit nights.

The Dake House

Some spirits choose to remain in familiar territory rather than move on. But what happens to all their treasured possessions left behind? Some are left to friends and relatives. Others end up cluttering the shelves of antique stores, which might be the reason so many antique stores are seemingly haunted.

The Antiques Plus shop in Genoa has at least three ghostly residents. Located in the circa-1870 home of Genoa's first undertaker, C. W. Dake, the shop was more recently the residence of a local widow. When she died, her daughter saw the building's possibilities and converted the little house to an antique store filled with an array of treasures from bygone days.

There are quilts, sparkling crystal glassware, exquisite needlework, and brightly colored 1950s dinnerware. But the centerpiece of the shop is the mysterious haunted painting. The lovely, unsigned still life of vibrant pink roses was a favorite of the owner's late mother. Many people have inquired about buying the painting, and for a while the owner entertained the idea of selling it. Then she noticed that the painting would fall from the wall whenever a prospective buyer expressed serious interest in purchasing it. At first she thought the nail that it hung on was loose. It wasn't. Then she checked the back of the painting to make sure the frame was securely held together. Nothing was amiss. Satisfied, she rehung the painting and forgot about it.

A few weeks later a woman came into the shop and was immediately drawn to the painting.

"I must have it," she announced. "How much?"

After a price was agreed upon, the buyer pulled out her credit card. "This will look lovely in my bedroom," she said. At that moment the painting crashed to the floor with a thud.

"Okay!" the shop owner said. "I think someone is trying to tell me something. I am sorry but the painting is not for sale."

This apparently appeased the specter. The painting has not fallen since. When Tom and Lisa Butler, directors of the Association TransCommunication, heard about the painting, their interests were piqued. The Butlers had seen similar paintings at the Golden Gate Spiritualist Church in San Francisco and believed it might be a "spirit painting." Spirit paintings, said to be created by departed spirits, were popular during the early-twentieth-century heyday of Spiritualism. The Butlers wanted to know more about this mysterious work of art.

The owner of the Dake House told the Butlers that her mother had been a friend of Reverend Florence Becker, founder of the Golden Gate Spiritualist Church. But she wasn't sure how, or when, her mother acquired the painting. After closely examining the painting, the Butlers felt it was a copy of a spirit painting, not an original, but nonetheless wanted to buy it. Their offers, like others before them, were met with a firm no. The mysterious haunted painting remains hanging in the pink room that closely matches the color of the painting's roses. And the shop remains peaceful.

But there are other ghosts on the premises. One bright summer morning, a man and his daughter arrived at the shop. They browsed the first floor and then climbed the stairs in search of other treasures. After spending considerable time in the attic rooms, the man paused at the window. Admiring the scene before him, he remarked, "What a beautiful view this is."

Without warning, he was slapped on the back of the head.

"Why did you do that?" he asked aloud, believing his daughter had hit him.

That's when he discovered that no one else was in the room. He'd heard the ghost stories about the place, but until this moment, he'd dismissed them as silly. Now he wasn't so sure. He scrambled down the stairs to find his daughter sitting on the porch.

"Let's go," he said.

The young lady took one look at her father and gasped. "What happened to you?"

"I think I may have just encountered a ghost," he said.

Perhaps the prankster ghost was responsible. The prankster keeps busy by toppling the shop's artificial flowers, tilting paintings, and occasionally playing with the fuses. A less likely suspect is the ghostly young woman who has been spotted by the stairs numerous times.

On a recent rainy afternoon, several people were browsing in the shop when the lights began to flicker on and off. The power finally went out altogether and the gloominess of the day intensified. Convinced it was nothing but a blown fuse, the owner ran out to the fuse box armed with a flashlight and new fuses. But there were no blown fuses.

"I'm not sure what happened," she explained back inside the shop.

"Is this place haunted?" someone asked.

The owner acknowledged that it was.

"Then it must be your ghost who's responsible."

At that very moment, as if on cue, the lights suddenly flickered back on again—another unexplained happening in a house where the spirits appear to have found a home.

Genoa Courthouse Museum

Genoa was the Douglas County seat in 1865 when the courthouse was built. This status lasted forty-nine years. By 1916 the nearby town of Minden outnumbered Genoa in population and had surpassed it in growth as well. Minden became the new Douglas County seat. The courthouse would see no more courtroom drama, but it would not stand empty either. Area children needed a school, so the courthouse was converted. It would serve as a school until 1956. In 1969 the courthouse opened as a museum operated by the Carson Valley Historical Society.

The old ground-floor jail has an interesting history, and possibly a ghost. In 1897, when an angry mob stormed the building and dragged Adam Uber from his cell and on to his lynching, the terrified man issued a curse against those responsible and their descendants (see page 39). And indeed there may still be something eerie about this jail. A local couple took their five-year-old granddaughter to the museum one Saturday morning and planned to picnic across the street at the old Mormon Station afterward. Those plans were changed when the five year old went back to the jail. The little girl took one look inside and went screaming out the door.

"What is it, dear?" the puzzled grandmother asked.

"The man! He is not nice!"

"Here let's go inside and I'll show you there is nothing to be afraid of," the grandmother offered.

The child pulled away, crying. "No, no, no. I don't want to go in there. He will get me!"

Neither grandparent had a clue what had frightened the little girl so. The grandfather went in and came out smiling: "The jail cell is dark and secured by an old iron door, and then there is the mannequin."

He turned to the little girl. "Was the man lying down?"

"He had something around his neck . . . and he was bleeding," she answered.

"Sounds like a gruesome mannequin to me," her grandmother remarked.

"That was not the mannequin," the grandfather replied.

Later that afternoon they asked a docent, who'd never heard such a story. But the little girl was adamant that there was a "bad man" in the jail.

Another incident occurred years ago when a caretaker was working in the museum late one evening. She heard someone coming down the stairs.

"The door was locked and I knew I was the only person in the building," the caretaker told me in an interview. "So naturally I was more than a little bit curious when I heard the sound of footsteps . . . someone was walking down the stairs. I looked up from my desk, thinking that a cat had somehow managed to get in. 'Who's there?' I called out. Not a sound. I looked through the museum only to discover what I'd known all along. No one was in the building but me."

Along with the occasional sighting of a spectral child, visitors to the museum have told of hearing ghostly children's laughter in the downstairs area where a long-ago classroom might have been. With the surging popularity of ghosts and ghost-hunting, some ghost investigations have taken place in the old courthouse. Most investigators agree that the building does have its resident ghosts. But none are sure just who these resident specters are.

The CVIC Hall and Flight 901A

The weather in Nevada's mountains is always unpredictable. It was especially so on March 1, 1964, when the worst aviation disaster in the Carson Valley's history occurred. That morning Paradise Airlines Flight 901A had taken off from Oakland en route to Tahoe Valley Airport, 149 miles away. The plane was full with four crewmen and eighty-one passengers headed for a weekend of fun and gambling as part of a skiing junket.

A late winter storm was raging along the California coast; snow was falling in the Sierra Nevada. Visibility was limited. As high winds swept into the region, the tower at Lake Tahoe informed the crew that there was zero visibility at the airport. The pilot replied that he was "holding over Tahoe." His last transmission was brief: "Flight 901 . . ." Then the radio tower lost communication.

The aircraft had slammed into Genoa Peak three miles east of Kingsbury Grade, killing everyone on board. According to experts, the plane would have cleared the mountain ridge had it been flying a mere three hundred feet higher. There was no voice recorder onboard, but later as investigators combed through the wreckage they discovered a problem with the plane's altimeter.

The next morning the snow-covered wreckage was located by search-and-rescue teams. This would not be a rescue mission, but rather one of recovery. The difficult task of locating the bodies and bringing them down the mountain began.

The tiny nearby town of Minden served as operations headquarters. The Carson Valley Improvement Club (CVIC) Hall, which had been a movie theater and a venue for proms and weddings, would now be utilized as a makeshift morgue. Most of the bodies were taken to the CVIC Hall for identification by friends and family. It would be three weeks before all were recovered. Shortly afterward the ghost stories began. Supposedly the CVIC Hall is haunted by one of the victims of Flight 901A, a man whose body was the last to arrive at the hall.

The man has stayed on here in Minden, making his presence known through mischievous little pranks. Nothing serious, mind you—just cold breezes, items being moved from one place to another, and other typical ghostly behavior.

Nevada State Museum

In 1857 the threat of war with the United States loomed over Mormon leader Brigham Young and his followers. All hands would be needed to aid in the potential fight, so he called his faithful settlers home to Salt Lake. As part of their preparations to return to Salt Lake, the settlers sold their lands in Genoa and the surrounding area at ridiculously low prices. The land that couldn't be sold was left up for grabs.

When word of the cheap land available in the Utah Territory reached Downieville, California, Abraham Curry saw opportunity. Along with his son, Charles, and his friends Frank Proctor and John Musser, Abraham Curry set out for Genoa, arriving in 1858. Taken with the area's beauty and its proximity to the rugged Sierra, Curry set his sights on a particular lot and offered its owners what he considered a fair price.

The owners, however, wanted more. Curry, a shrewd businessman, thought the $1,000 asking price was ridiculously inflated, but he wanted that lot. So he made a counteroffer. The owners wouldn't budge. When he finally realized that an agreement could not be reached, Curry said, "Well then, I will build a city of my own." With those words he headed north toward an area known as Eagle Valley.

At the time of Curry's arrival, Eagle Valley was little more than a trading post and ranch operated by a group of men who had settled the area in 1851. Curry stopped and looked around at the valley, which had been named for a magnificent eagle that had once soared overhead; now the eagle's body and its fine feathers decorated the door of the trading post. Envisioning a thriving city, Curry and his friends eagerly purchased several acres. Abraham Curry is known today as the founder of Carson City.

Curry's ghostly presence is said to reside at the Nevada State Museum, which is housed in a building that was the United States

Mint until 1893. Curry was the mint's first superintendent, and the walls were built of stone from a quarry Curry owned. His ghost is believed to roam the museum just to make sure that everything is as it should be. Those who have encountered him say there is no reason to be afraid, as he is a friendly sort of spirit.

Only one death occurred in the building during its time as the mint from 1869 to 1893. This fatal accident happened on the morning of December 12, 1872, and involved a man named Osborne Parker. He was working alone in the basement when his sweater somehow got tangled in the equipment. Parker's predicament was hopeless. His bloodcurdling screams could be heard throughout the building, but help was too late in reaching him. He was crushed before rescuers could get to him and extricate him from the machinery. Osborne Parker's ghost is believed to be responsible for unexplained noises, lights that flicker off and on, and loud stomping footsteps. Those who have worked in the building after hours tell of being startled by an elevator that travels from floor to floor of its own accord. These are all classic signs of a haunting.

Perhaps Curry and Parker are not alone here in the museum. After all, some of Nevada's treasures and its history are housed here. One never knows what other ghosts may have come along with the relics.

Orson Hyde's Curse

Orson Hyde was one of the faithful who chose to obey Brigham Young's call to return to Salt Lake in order to defend the settlement against possible U.S. Army action. In order to do so, he would have to leave his sawmill and other land holdings behind. With time of the essence, Hyde struck a deal with Jacob Rose, who was to rent the property. When the morning of his departure came, Hyde reluctantly left the Carson Valley, still expecting to receive fair payment for his property.

Five years passed. Orson Hyde realized that he wasn't going to be paid for his holdings, and angrily issued his curse with the following letter to those residing in the area:

> January 27, 1862. To the People of Carson and Washoe Valleys. Ladies and Gentlemen, Not quite seven years ago I was sent to

your district as Probate Judge of Carson County, with powers and instructions from executive of this Territory to organize your district into a county under the laws of Utah—those valleys being then the lawful and rightful field of Utah's jurisdiction. But opposition on your part to the measure was unceasingly made in almost every form, both trivial and important, open and secret. Your allies in California were ever ready to second your opposition of whatever character or in whatever shape.

In the year following (1856, I think) Mr. Price and myself built a valuable saw mill in Washoe Valley, made and purchased several land claims there for ourselves and our friends—made considerable improvements thereon; but being called away on short notice, this property, then worth $10,000, was rented to Jacob Rose for a limited term, at a stipulated price. On this rent he advanced one span of small, indifferent mules, an old worn-out harness, two yokes of oxen and an old wagon. This is all that we have ever received for the use of our property in that valley though we have sent bills for goods or merchandise. But no response, except on paper, and even that not of the most encouraging kind . . .

Warming to his subject, Hyde went on to warn the people of Washoe Valley just what would befall them.

You shall be visited of the Lord of Hosts with thunder and with earthquakes and with floods, with pestilence and famine until your names are not known amongst men for you have rejected the authority of God, trampled upon his laws and his ordinances, and given yourselves up to serve the god of this world; to rioting in debauchery, in abominations, drunkenness and corruption.

Orson Hyde's curse was blamed for the Washoe Valley flood of 1880, and is still cited as the reason for mudslides, fires, and any other natural disasters that befall this region.

Orion Clemens Home

Samuel Clemens was born in Hannibal, Missouri. But Nevadans like to point out that Mark Twain was born right here in the Silver State. They only disagree as to whether it was in Carson City or Virginia City that he first took the nom de plume. For the sake of this tale, let us assume that it was in Carson City where Clemens chose the name Mark Twain.

We do know that Abraham Lincoln was indirectly responsible for Clemens coming westward in the first place. In 1861 when President Lincoln appointed James Nye as Nevada's territorial governor, he also appointed a young politician by the name of Orion Clemens to the post of secretary of the territory. Knowing that his wife and young daughter could not accompany him to Nevada, Orion Clemens invited his younger brother Samuel to join him on the long journey west.

The Clemens brothers arrived in Carson City shortly after James Nye. Orion quickly went to work on his political career and Samuel decided to try his hand at mining in Aurora, eighty miles south. The work was more grueling than he had imagined and offered little reward. Disappointment set in, and the younger Clemens grew bored and restless. Later he would claim to have walked all the way back to Carson City from Aurora, but knowing his propensity for exaggeration, not every historian accepts that tale. Back in Carson City, he covered politics before moving up to Virginia City where he hoped to find work at the *Territorial Enterprise* newspaper.

After penning several quick-witted letters to the editor, Clemens landed the job and embarked on his writing career. Back in Carson City, Orion continued to assist Governor Nye. Since Nye wasn't fond of the area and was frequently in San Francisco on business, many of the duties of governor fell to Orion. In fact, he was often referred to as "acting governor." He enjoyed entertaining but needed a suitable house once his wife Mollie and daughter Jennie came from Iowa to join him. In 1863 he spent thousands to have the perfect house built at 502 N. Division Street at its intersection with Spear Street. The little Clemens family was happy in their new home in Carson City, where they entertained many famous and influential people of the day, which by this time included Orion's brother.

Twain was an indulgent uncle who adored his little niece. When he discovered she was soliciting donations for her church, he presented a fundraising speech at the Carson City courthouse and gave all the money raised to the church. Less than a week later Jennie would be struck with spotted fever. Her parents and uncle sat by her bedside until the end. When she died, they were inconsolable.

All Carson City mourned kindhearted little Jennie, who had been saving her own pennies to buy a bible for the church. A new bible was purchased in her memory.

Jennie was Orion and Mollie's only child. They had doted on her. The grief-stricken Clemenses buried Jennie at Lone Mountain Cemetery and vowed never to have another child. Despite all their entertaining and their expensive home, the Clemenses were not wealthy people and they faced financial hardship brought on by the cost of their child's funeral and coffin. This, and grief at the loss of his beloved niece, may explain Mark Twain's anger at the local undertaker in Carson City.

Twain voiced his condemnation with a letter to the *Territorial Enterprise*, dated February 12, 1864:

Concerning Undertakers.

There is a system of extortion going on here which is absolutely terrific, and I wonder why the Carson Independent has never ventilated the subject. There seems to be only one undertaker in the town, and he owns the only graveyard in which it is at all high-toned or aristocratic to be buried. Consequently, when a man loses his wife or his child, or his mother, this undertaker makes him sweat for it. I appeal to those whose firesides death has made desolate during the few fatal weeks just past, if I am not speaking the truth. Does not this undertaker take advantage of that unfortunate delicacy which prevents a man from disputing an unjust bill for services rendered in burying the dead, to extort ten-fold more than his labors are worth? . . . This undertaker charges a hundred and fifty dollars for a pine coffin that cost him twenty or thirty, and fifty dollars for a grave that did not cost him ten—and this at a time when his ghastly services are required at least seven times a week. I gather these facts from some of the best citizens of Carson, and I can publish their names at any moment if you want them. What Carson needs is a few more undertakers—there is vacant land enough here for a thousand cemeteries.

The *Independent* fought back the next day with the following editorial:

Our friend, Mark Twain, is such a joker that we cannot tell when he is really in earnest. He says in his last letter to the ENTERPRISE, that our undertaker charges exorbitantly for his services—as much as $150 for a pine coffin and $50 for a grave and is astonished that the Independent has not, ere this, said something about this extortion. As yet we have had no occasion for a coffin or a bit of ground for grave purposes, and therefore know nothing about the price of such things. If any of our citizens think they have been imposed upon in this particular, it is their duty to ventilate the matter. We have heard no complaints.

Twain responded in the *Territorial Enterprise*:

That first sentence is false, and that clause in the second, which refers to the Independent, is false, also. I knew better than to be astonished when I wrote it. Unfortunately for the public of Carson, both propositions in the third sentence are true. Having had no use for a coffin himself, the editor "therefore knows nothing about the price of such things." It is my unsolicited opinion that he knows very little about anything. And anybody who will read his paper calmly and dispassionately for a week will endorse that opinion. And more especially his knowing nothing about Carson, is not surprising; he seldom mentions that town in his paper. If the Second advent were to occur here, you would hear of it first in some other newspaper.

The editor of the Independent says he don't know anything about this undertaker business. If he would go and report a while for some responsible newspaper, he would learn the knack of finding out things.

The *Independent* apologized to Mark Twain and Carson City founder Abraham Curry paid for Jennie's simple headstone. The Clemenses sold the home that had once brought them so much joy, and moved back to Iowa. They never returned to Nevada.

Like so many other of the city's historic homes, the Clemens home has been converted to law offices. The upstairs bedroom where little Jennie Clemens died faces Division Street. Some claim to see the specter of a child in the window late at night when the building is otherwise unoccupied. Over the years, sightings of the little girl's ghost have occurred in other areas of the house and at the Lone Mountain Cemetery where she is buried.

Lone Mountain Cemetery

According to Nevada cemetery expert Cindy Southerland in her book *Cemeteries of Carson City and Carson Valley*, Lone Mountain Cemetery is a compilation of several other Carson City cemeteries. As a rule, cemeteries aren't very haunted; those interred in cemeteries had little or no connection to the place in life, and the burial grounds are typically not the scenes of tragic death. There are exceptions to every rule, though, and Lone Mountain is one such exception. Ghost hunters believe it is haunted.

Little Jennie Clemens, who was ten when she died, is one of those ghostly residents. Her heartbroken parents left Nevada after her death. And one might think that without any family to tend her grave, the spectral child would be anxious when encountered. Not so, say those who've witnessed her happily skipping through the cemetery. Recently a plaque was placed near the child's simple marker and reads "You are not alone Jennie/ your Presbyterian sisters/ cherish your bible."

Another resident is Hank Monk, a stagecoach driver from Nevada's early days. Legends have been built around him. One involves the wild ride over the Sierra he shared with visiting newspaperman Horace Greeley (of "Go west, young man" fame). Greeley, so the story goes, made the mistake of telling Hank that he was pressed for time. As the coach raced over the mountain passes Greeley became frightened. But Hank was not one to back down from a challenge or a promise.

"Keep your seat, Horace," he called down to his frightened passenger. "I'll get you there on time!"

And he did. Horace Greeley never forgot or forgave Hank Monk for his part in helping to spread the story of his discomfiture during the harrowing coach ride. Popular wisdom was that the story had made Greeley look foolish, costing him a political nomination.

As much as Greeley despised Monk, the public loved him and his heroics. Commemorating the daring feat of the local hero, local composer John Meder wrote the "Hank Monk Schottische" in 1878. (A *schottische* is a slow polka.) Hank's career as a stagecoach driver was long behind him when he died of pneumonia at the age of fifty-seven. Some said he had lost his ability to maneuver a team around the twisting mountain passes, in part because of his heavy drinking. Others believed age had slowed the reflexes of the expert driver. The truth was probably somewhere in the middle. It didn't matter to Hank's many friends, who threw him a grand funeral on February 28, 1883. A large crowd gathered to pay last respects to the colorful man who'd bravely done what many could not. Hank had been a hero.

Reverend G. Davis stepped to the pulpit and offered the eulogy: "The man who knows his own natural capacities and strives to occupy the position in life best suited to his gifts, however humble, is a man of brains and honest purpose. Too much credit cannot be given a man who follows a humble calling and takes an honest pride in doing all his work well." At the conclusion of the funeral mourners followed the carriage containing Hank Monk's earthly remains as it slowly made its way to Lone Mountain Cemetery.

Within a month of his funeral the ghostly Hank Monk was seen in his favorite old rocker pulled up to the potbelly stove at the Ormsby House on Carson Street in Carson City. Some there tested the veracity of the sightings by moving the chair to another part of the room. The next day the rocker was again near the stove. For many years afterward old Hank was said to haunt the premises. His phantom was occasionally seen quietly guzzling his drink by more than one patron at the bar where the original Ormsby House once stood.

Hank's bones may be buried in Lone Mountain Cemetery, but his ghost is on the move. With his former haunt of the Ormsby House now gone, his phantom is sometimes spotted by patrons of another local bar. These witnesses have had one too many toddies perhaps, but then again Hank was known to challenge the impossible. He is said to hang out in Lone Mountain Cemetery when not occupying a stool at one of the saloons.

One night ghost hunters conducted an investigation at Lone Mountain Cemetery. Armed with flashlights and cameras, they first stood by Jennie Clemens's grave before moving on to Hank Monk's final resting place. It was a bone-chilling night—not the sort that would deter a ghost, but certainly one that had these intrepid ghost-seekers shivering in their down parkas. Ready to end the hunt, they headed for their cars. For some reason they decided to stop at the

Soldier Memorial, which marks the plot where men from Fort Churchill were reburied when their bodies were disinterred and brought here to the cemetery in 1884. According to a person who was there that night, the statue of the soldier that tops the monument glided down from the memorial and started marching toward the east, which would make sense: Fort Churchill State Historical Park is forty miles east of Carson City.

The specter of a marching soldier might have been enough to send the ghost hunters running, but it's not the strangest story to come from Lone Mountain Cemetery. That would have to be the tale of grave robbing that took place in 2000.

Human skulls apparently bring good money on some markets, attached ghosts notwithstanding of course. The crafty entrepreneur/grave robber saw a need and decided to fill it. She broke into the strange-looking crypt of early-day Nevada pioneer P. H. Clayton and his wife, Helen. The crypt bears the words "Our Home." This meant nothing to the grave robber. She was intent on making some extra cash so she spent several hours that night sawing at the skulls of the Claytons. She was later caught trying to sell her ill-gotten loot and sentenced for her crime. In describing the crime, the local newspapers shared the macabre detail that one of the skulls still had a few strands of brown hair attached to it. The skulls were returned and the crypt was sealed. Let's hope that the Claytons are once again resting in peace in their home.

Rinckel Mansion

In 1875 Carson City businessman Mathias Rinckel spared no expense in having his fine mansion built at 102 N. Curry Street. While there were no fireplaces, there was every other convenience of the time. Rinckel's home was one of the area's first to have indoor plumbing. After he and his wife died, their daughter Louise took possession of the home. She lived alone there until her death. After being sold a number of times, the house was converted to the Carlson House Restaurant. But Louise was apparently not very happy with the restaurant. Patrons and employees of the Carlson House told of full liquor bottles being toppled by unseen hands, glasses crashing to the floor, and lights flickering on and off. During important sporting events a rush of cold air would billow through the bar and the big-screen televisions would come unplugged.

"There was no earthly explanation for it to happen," a former employee said.

No explanation other than the fact that the bar was in Louise's former bedroom. A teetotaler, she may not have taken kindly to the idea of alcohol being served in the room where she entered and exited the world.

The restaurant has long since been closed and the mansion converted to the Donald W. Reynolds Press Center. Hopefully Louise likes the building's current incarnation better than she did the restaurant.

Governor's Mansion

The state of Nevada's birthday falls on Halloween, October 31. This is why the Governor's Mansion in Carson City is lavishly decorated with ghosts, goblins, and all manner of monsters every October. Regardless of which party is in power, it's a long-held Carson City tradition that the governor dispenses candy to trick-or-treaters and well-wishers on the front steps of the mansion every Halloween night.

The state's first ten governors did not have an official residence; it wasn't until forty-five years after the state was admitted to the Union that the idea of a governor's house was brought up in legislation. If had been left up to Governor John Sparks, who was in office at the time, the state's top executive would not have an official residence. Fortunately for those who came later, Sparks was vetoed and the selection of a location began. Governor Sparks died in office in 1908 and wouldn't live to see the new mansion completed the next year. Lieutenant Governor Denver Dickerson assumed the governor's duties and he and his wife, Una, moved into the new mansion.

On the evening of January 1, 1910, Governor Dickerson and the first lady proudly held an open house so residents of Nevada could get a good look at the new mansion. With a winter storm raging across the Carson Valley, strong winds swept down from the Sierra. Icy sleet pelted the capital city, knocking out the mansion's power. Undeterred, the governor and Mrs. Dickerson received their visitors

by gaslight. Later everyone would remember how the glow of gaslight lent a charming ambiance to the evening and how elegant the first lady was in her embroidered crepe de chine gown.

Una Dickerson loved the mansion. She was the first governor's wife who was actually born in the state, and she is the only first lady believed to haunt the mansion. Her ghost has been seen walking on the mansion's landing several times over the years. But there are other ghosts here, as well as disembodied voices. The most popular and perhaps unusual spirit is the ghostly presence who resides in the antique grandfather clock. It seems this spirit became quite active when the clock was moved from the state capitol building to the Governor's Mansion. Those who've witnessed the ghostly goings-on say that the air around the clock suddenly turns icy and the door of the clock will sometimes swing open of its own accord. A former caretaker at the mansion told of going downstairs late one night and noticing that the clock's door was opened. She closed the door snugly and was surprised when it suddenly snapped open. "I really wasn't frightened, but I didn't try to close it again," she said.

The apparitions of a young woman and a child are sometimes spotted on the expansive staircase. There is also the ghostly presence of a man who is dressed in a style of long ago. Some say he is Fred Balzar, the only Nevada governor to die in the mansion. Then again, he could be one of the former governors who never had the privilege of living in the stately home. The ghostly residents of the mansion are the perfect houseguests, regardless of their political party. Not constrained by term limits, these ghosts are happy to reside in the mansion year after year, term after term.

Smail House

In 1862 carpenter James Smail built a house on a Carson City lot he had purchased for $250. A few months later he sold the house at a considerable profit. Today the Smail House, at the corner of Robinson and Curry Streets, is often featured on Carson City's annual Ghost Walk. Like so many other homes in the city's historic district, the Smail House now houses commercial businesses. Revelations, an eclectic shop that specializes in costume sales and rentals, has occupied the Smail House for a number of years. If there's a ghost on the premises, it seems to be the playful sort. Items have been known to topple from shelves for no apparent reason.

On a crisp autumn afternoon, three young women stopped in the shop looking for costumes to wear to the Nevada Day Parade. As they rummaged through the dresses, one of them turned from her friends' idle conversation to admire the lovely taffeta dress another patron was wearing.

"I never will forget her," the woman said. "The dress had a cream-color bodice and the skirt was wine with tiny cream stripes. It fit her so well, as if it had been specially tailored for her. I was just about to tell her so, when she suddenly raised a hand to her face and vanished into thin air. I didn't tell the others what I had seen."

I'll Come Back if I Can

It well could be that the ghost of John Murphy still wanders the streets of Carson City. Murphy, a believer in Spiritualism, hoped to return to the city after his death, and announced his intentions to do so shortly before he was hanged at the foot of Lone Mountain on December 29, 1874. Addressing the crowd that had gathered to watch him die, Murphy said, "I'll come back if I can. When you hear them chains rattling, look out for me."

John Murphy had arrived in Carson City seven months earlier, a man with a grudge and a gun. On the morning of May 12, 1874, he was leaving the St. Charles Hotel when he looked across the street at the Ormsby House and saw John McCallum. The memory rushed back of the recent beating he had suffered at McCallum's hands during a fight at a mining camp. It mattered little that Murphy had struck the first blow; he still seethed with anger. "Stop there McCallum," he called as he crossed the street.

Fear spread across McCallum's face. "Please don't shoot me," he begged the murderous Murphy.

When he realized his words were falling on deaf ears, McCallum turned from his assailant and fled down the street. Murphy followed close on his heels. When cornered, the unfortunate McCallum again pleaded with Murphy to spare him. Murphy replied with a bullet.

The wounded man yelled, "Murder!" and then staggered down Carson Street. He was taken to a local doctor's home, but his injuries were beyond repair. He suffered in agony for two days before death mercifully released him. John Murphy was taken into custody for the murder.

At John Murphy's trial Thomas Wells, witness for the prosecution, testified:

> That [McCallum] did not at the first difficulty at the camp nor at any previous time give the defendant any occasion to assault deceased as he did. Deceased stated that he came to Carson from the camps on Sunday afternoon. That the reason he left the camps and came to this town was because he wanted to evade Murphy; that just previous to leaving he was informed that Murphy had returned there. He also said that at the time of shooting he had no weapon upon his person. This is a statement of what he said as fully as I can give it.

John Murphy was convicted of the killing. He appealed his conviction to the Nevada Supreme Court and lost. On the morning of his execution, Murphy thumped his book on Spiritualism and addressed the crowd, "This is my doom, but this book teaches me that I will never die." In an attempt to explain the murder for which he was about to be executed, Murphy said, "When Johnny Murphy draws, he draws to kill."

He then read from his book on Spiritualism:

> I have never kneeled before, but I do kneel now. Almighty and most merciful Father, who has created us in thy wisdom and sustained us by thy love, look down with compassion on this thy unhappy child now present, and assist him, we beseech thee, in his search after truth.
>
> Roll from his mind the clouds of error, ignorance and superstition, that the light of thy wisdom may shine upon him, cheering his heart, enlightening his understanding, and rendering bright his pathway to thy holy mansions eternal in the heavens. Suffer thy holy spirits to minister unto him as his guardians and guides, to lead him from darkness to light and place him on the plane of everlasting progression.

With those words, the condemned man asked for chewing tobacco and then said, "I am ready now. I have suffered a great deal gentlemen. And I would like to give them judges a little drop if ever I come back."

According to those who have seen the ghost of Murphy wandering Carson Street, John Murphy has indeed come back to the area where he met his demise.

Don't Challenge the 601

Nevada's early days were filled with violence. Secret vigilante groups like the 601 often took it upon themselves to ensure the safety of their families and fellow citizens. Anyone deemed dangerous or a threat to the community was ordered to leave town or suffer the consequences; these consequences usually proved fatal. A stern warning from the dreaded 601 was often enough to send even the most dangerous killer packing—but not always.

Tom Burt was given to pyromania. The fires he started posed a danger to life and limb of the citizens of Carson City—the city's wooden buildings could go up in flames in a matter of minutes. When Carson City's 601 decided that Burt should leave town, the young man refused to do so.

Burt slept at the firehouse, which is where members of the 601 roused him one night. Burt had been given his chance to leave town. His refusal would cost him his life. He was dragged to the Lone Mountain Cemetery, where a rope was thrown over the gate and Burt was hanged. Tom Burt would set no more fires.

Early the next morning a graveyard caretaker discovered his lifeless body at the entrance of the cemetery. The corpse was a reminder to all those who didn't abide by the law: the 601 was watching.

Some believe that Tom Burt has had the last laugh. Since that cold December night so long ago, his apparition has been spotted in the area of Curry Street near the old firehouse. Unlike some specters that appear miserable and unhappy, Tom Burt smiles merrily. Apparently the power of the 601 only extended so far.

Gold and Silver Country

UNLIKE THE FERTILE VALLEYS OF NEIGHBORING CALIFORNIA, NEVADA IS mostly desert. Little grows save sagebrush and other drought-tolerant plants. The state's forbidding terrain might have been ignored by settlers if not for the discovery of silver. By 1859 California's gold rush had ended and miners started to look elsewhere for the opportunity to strike it rich. They found it in Nevada near present-day Virginia City. The Comstock Lode, one of the richest mining discoveries in our country's history, would yield close to $50 million in silver ore.

Some people became millionaires overnight. Others were not so fortunate. Life was hard and crime rates were high in the boom towns. Murder and suicide were commonplace on the Comstock. Smaller discoveries of silver were found from time to time, but the Comstock Lode was all but played out by 1874 and people left the state in droves.

Then, in 1900, Jim Butler was looking for a lost burro when he discovered gold and silver in the central Nevada desert near Tonopah. Within a few years gold would be discovered near present-day Goldfield. The rush was on once again. Most of the those brought to the area by the ore strikes have long since left, but if the region's ghost stories are to be believed, quite a few of them are still hanging around.

The Goldfield Hotel

Ask any ghost hunter what's on their bucket list of haunted sites to explore, and chances are the Goldfield Hotel in Goldfield will be on that list. This old hotel is considered by many to be Nevada's most haunted site. If we are to accept what popular TV ghost-hunting shows tell us, the hotel is teeming with ghostly activity. Built in 1908, when Goldfield was Nevada's largest town, the brick hotel that stands on the corner of Crook and Columbia Streets is actually the third incarnation of the Goldfield Hotel. The other two burned to the ground. And that leads us to our first two of the hotel's ghostly residents.

Judge J. M. Ellis was traveling to his home in Denver, Colorado. Anthony Heber was a bespectacled salesman from Southern California. Sometime during their 1906 stay the Goldfield Hotel caught fire and neither of them was able to escape the flames. The coroner conducted his inquest there in the ashes of the hotel. Offering up the burned and severed skulls of Heber and Ellis as evidence, he carefully and in graphic detail explained how the unfortunate men came to their deaths.

Hope springs eternal and soon another, grander, Goldfield Hotel was built. No expense was spared in its construction. The hotel included a large restaurant, two bars that offered the finest champagne, a billiard room, and a barbershop. Every room was richly carpeted and had its own telephone that was connected to a central switchboard. Rich velvet draperies covered the windows and exquisite tile adorned the lobby. Sadly, the hotel's heyday wouldn't last. The gold gave out and the crowds moved on, leaving the hotel a ghost, abandoned in the desert. With fewer guests each week, the hotel finally closed its doors forever just after World War II.

Since then numerous businesspeople have come to Goldfield hoping to restore the hotel to its former glory with an eye toward reopening it. All such attempts have met with failure. Some say it's as if the building is cursed. Others say there are just too many ghosts in the hotel. And those ghosts, especially that of George Wingfield, don't want company.

Wingfield was Nevada's wealthiest, and thus most powerful, man in the early twentieth century. He ruled the roost in Goldfield and was part owner of the Goldfield Hotel for a short time. According to ghost-hunting legend, Wingfield haunts the hotel and can become angry and hostile to those he doesn't like. His ethereal cigar smoke wafts through the building, warning of his presence. Some of Wingfield's anger may be justified. He is said to be the villain in the story of the Goldfield Hotel's most famous ghost, Elizabeth.

Elizabeth was a young prostitute who fell in love with George Wingfield. When she revealed that she was pregnant with his child, Wingfield forced her to go to the hotel, where he kept her chained to a radiator in Room 109. That's the generally accepted story. But it gets worse. Depending on who is telling the tale, Elizabeth gave birth and was either murdered by Wingfield or starved to death by him. He then callously threw the child down a mineshaft under the hotel. The beautiful Elizabeth has haunted Room 109 ever since.

Virginia Ridgway has been the caretaker of the Goldfield Hotel for more than thirty years. She doesn't necessarily believe the entire Elizabeth story, but she believes that the ghostly young woman haunts Room 109. Virginia regularly brings flowers and presents to the ghost in Room 109. She is protective of her ghost, and cautions her ghost-hunting friends that although they are free to take photographs and record EVP, they must never use flash in this area; the lights are said to startle Elizabeth.

Virginia likes to take people upstairs to what she calls the "energy room," where it is claimed one can feel the energy that is in the hotel. Local ghost hunters believe the building is a portal through which ghosts enter and exit the earthly plane. Interestingly enough, the energy room is the same area where Heber and Ellis met their deaths in the earlier hotel fire.

Some psychics say that the Goldfield Hotel's basement is the hotel's most haunted area. This is where a ghostly man clad in jeans and leather jacket is encountered. The specter does not respect personal space. He will stand very close to witnesses at times. An investigator who saw him told the following story:

> There were a lot of us down there in the basement. I didn't have any idea what group he was with, only that he was standing much too close to me. I turned to my friend and asked, "Who's he?" She shrugged her shoulders like she didn't know what I was talking

about. [I said] "Okay, you need . . ." That's all I said. Before I could finish [the sentence] he was gone. He was right there next to me and then he wasn't. It was the weirdest thing.

The hotel is currently closed. No one is permitted inside without authorization. No one, that is, but the ghosts.

Goldfield High School

Nevada's dry desert climate is harsh on the state's historic buildings. This is especially evident at the old Goldfield High School. Built about the same time as the elegant brick Goldfield Hotel, the school was constructed of lumber, and has not withstood this cruel environment as well as the hotel has. Regular ghost-hunting fundraisers are conducted at the dilapidated old school and its owners are hopeful that with the help of federal grant money and private contributions the building can be saved and restored. Sadly, this will be an uphill battle. Time and climate have done much damage.

None of this seems to bother the ghosts who have taken up residence in the old school. Some of these ghosts may be connected to the bathroom sinks from the Goldfield Hotel, which are stored here. At least, this is what an investigating psychic believed. The woman was certain she was picking up the name of a child who came to the school along with the sinks. The little specter was lost and looking for someone. The psychic tried her best to convince the boy to either return to the hotel or leave our world behind and go into the light. His refusal was heart wrenching. How could he leave his sister here? he asked. The ghost was positive the sister was still here at the school. No contact could be made with her however.

If you stand at the staircase on a quiet and windless night, you just might hear the sounds of long-ago students racing up and down the stairs. Some investigators have captured EVP of the ghostly students' laughter and talk. More frightening than the ghosts are the bats. Occasionally they come swooping through the broken walls and crevices. It's enough to send even the most intrepid ghost hunter shrieking.

St. Mary's Art & Retreat Center

One of Virginia City's most beautiful buildings, the St. Mary's Art & Retreat Center, has an interesting past. Built on land that was donated by Louise Mackay, wife of wealthy Comstock mine owner John Mackay, St. Mary Louise Hospital was the first hospital in Virginia City.

Intended to serve the needs of the down-and-out as well as miners who could pay a small portion of their wages for the privilege of medical care, the hospital was also used to confine the insane. And this is where two of St. Mary's ghosts make their entrance.

There was a terrible fire at the hospital. As winds swept the flames upward in the building, nuns scurried about trying to save the sick and incapacitated from certain death. When one young nun realized that all but one person was safe, she ran back upstairs to save an insane man who had been chained to a wall. She was too late. He had perished in the flames. She died there trying to make her way back to safety.

The hospital closed in 1940. The building was renamed and repurposed as an arts center beginning in the mid-1960s. Art classes are offered at the stately old building during the spring and summer. Many of those who've attended have had encounters with the ghostly "White Nun." The lonely specter's attire is white, from head to toe. She walks the halls of St. Mary's, calmly checking on the welfare of her patients. Some say they can sense her presence in the chapel. She has been seen pushing a squeaking gurney down the long hallways, in Room 11, and forlornly looking out a second-story window. A former caretaker told of her encounter with the ghostly White Nun on the staircase several years ago: "She was not attempting to frighten anyone; she merely wanted to be seen."

The nun is kindly and doesn't want anyone getting cold. A few people have told of waking in the middle of the night to see the White Nun gently tucking the quilt up around them.

The wraith of the crazed man who died in the fire has also been felt in the attic area. His energy, psychics say, is not one of calm, but is rather unsettling. When art classes and events are not in session, paranormal conferences and ghost hunters often descend on the building. Gathering photos, psychic impressions, and electronic voice phenomena, they are convinced that the Art Center is haunted.

Beautiful Lena and the Ghosts of the Old Washoe Club

The Washoe Club is the center of ghostly goings-on in Virginia City. Boasting a museum dedicated to the paranormal and having hosted teams from Travel Channel's *Ghost Adventures* and SyFy's *Ghost Hunters*, the Washoe attracts paranormal investigators from around the world.

Numerous sightings and other such phenomena have occurred during all-night investigations of the upstairs area. Several people have reported being gently pushed or touched by one of the resident ghosts. But the ghostly man that has been described as a dark, negative energy is not so kindly. He stays in the upstairs rooms and was responsible, some say, for an investigator being shoved down the back stairs during a recent ghost investigation. During a séance in the upstairs area it was revealed that this man had murdered several people during his lifetime. For whatever reason he feels compelled to linger on at the Washoe Club.

There are other ghosts at the Washoe. One is of a little girl who was killed long ago when a runaway team of horses pulled a wagon down C Street. She's rarely seen, preferring to stay in the shadows; pitiful sobs announce her presence.

By far the most famous ghost in residence is that of beautiful Lena. Patrons at the downstairs bar have been shocked to look in the mirror and see a woman in blue staring back at them. She is believed to be the ghost of a beautiful young prostitute who died upstairs during the town's silver boom. Suicide or murder, no one is sure how Lena died, only that it was a violent death.

The Wahoe Club came into existence during a time when life was cheap and death was fast in early-day Virginia City. While some men became millionaires overnight in the Comstock Lode, most didn't. They worked long hours far beneath the earth and barely scraped by. Life was hard for men of the Comstock but it was worse on women, especially those who worked as prostitutes.

The Old Washoe was built in 1862 as a place for the town's movers and shakers to relax and unwind. During this time Lena was probably one of the women who entertained the Comstock's wealthiest men in the private club upstairs. Perhaps she made one of them

so angry that he strangled her, as some psychics have said. Or she may have fallen in love and realized the hopelessness of her situation, choosing poison as a way out of her misery. She is most often described as wearing blue; her favorite spots are the bar and near the spiral staircase. EVP of a woman's voice saying "poison" and "murder" was collected upstairs several years ago. During this investigation the sound of shattering glass was also recorded on an old reel-to-reel recorder. Was this a hint as to how Lena died, or perhaps a warning from the other side?

Piper's Opera House

On January 28, 1878, all of Virginia City was celebrating the opening of the opulent new Piper's Opera House. The assembled crowd believed Piper's was destined to become a cultural center for the city even finer than the previous opera house, which had been destroyed by fire a year earlier. President Ulysses S. Grant and Mark Twain were among the luminaries who attended performances at the opera house. This second incarnation of the opera house burned down in 1883. A third building, the one presently in use, was constructed at B and Union Streets in 1885.

When the silver played out, Virginia City's population dwindled. Beginning in 1920, the opera house fell silent and dark. It was reopened as a museum in 1940, and resumed theater operations in the 1970s. Every theater and opera house has its idiosyncrasies and its ghosts. It is fitting that most of the specters at Piper's are thought to be performers who long to return to the stage. A pretty redheaded actress learned about the opera house's ghostly Casanova when the mischievous spirit pinched her bottom one night. She was somewhat startled, but not frightened.

A ghostly woman who appears wearing a bottle-green dress and strands of pearls has been seen in the opera house countless times. She seems to be agitated and looking for someone or something. She walks back and forth from the front door to the stage. Rarely does she acknowledge the living. Perhaps she is the ghostly Julia Bulette, a long-ago courtesan who was strangled in her bed shortly after attending a play at Piper's.

The other female spirit, according to those who have encountered her, is not the friendly sort. Apparently she likes to be alone in the opera house. She is said to have pulled the hair of and pinched more than one visitor to Piper's.

Ghost hunters especially enjoy the haunted ambiance of Piper's Opera House. Several ghost investigations have taken place here at the theater, which is now owned by the nonprofit Piper's Opera House Programs. Depending on whom you talk to, the building may or may not be off-limits to ghost hunters. In either case, it's certainly not off-limits to ghosts.

Café del Rio

Everyone, including hungry ghost hunters, knows that some of the best Tex-Mex food in the Virginia City area is served at the Café del Rio. The popular eatery is housed in the old Werrin Building, which dates back to 1873. John Werrin, who had immigrated from Cornwall, England, operated a grocery store on the ground floor and rented the upstairs rooms to lodgers.

At least one of those lodgers has stayed on. Not much is known of her except that she was young and her name was Margaret. In her honor, the newly remodeled upstairs banquet room is known as Margaret's Room. The original brick wall remains, although the track lights are a decidedly twenty-first century addition. Nonetheless, they add a nice yesteryear glow. Diners upstairs can walk out onto the balcony during nice weather. During a full moon the view toward Sugar Loaf to the east offers a brief glimpse of how it was when John Werrin rented out these rooms so long ago. Margaret might have enjoyed this very same view. Of course, she looked down onto a very different C Street, one filled with horses and buggies. Whatever the changes, the ghostly Margaret seems to be very happy in her updated digs.

Before the Café del Rio opened, the building was used as rental housing. A family that resided there years ago claimed the sounds and aromas of frying bacon and percolating coffee wafted through their home at daybreak every morning.

"It was old man Werrin. I'm sure of that," the former resident said. "I caught a glimpse of an old man hovering over the stove one day . . . never saw him but the one time though."

Whoever the ghost was, that morning coffee sure seems like a thoughtful touch.

Silver State National Peace Officers Museum

The Silver State National Peace Officers Museum is located in back of the Storey County Courthouse. It is a fitting tribute to the brave men and women who help keep us safe. Given that the museum is housed in the old Storey County Jail, it's possible that the resident ghosts here include both good guys and bad guys.

During ghost investigations at the museum people have reported feeling extremely cold even in warm weather. Some ghost hunters have reportedly been grabbed or felt nauseous and fearful in the cell area. At least one investigator claimed she was scratched on her back while sitting in a cell alone trying to collect EVP. A volunteer who does not believe in ghosts had a very strange experience one morning when he came in to find that all the officers' coats on display had been tossed off their hangers and thrown on the floor. He wondered why on earth anyone would do this. When the night volunteer came to work he asked him about it.

"I don't know what you're talking about," the night volunteer said. "Every one of those coats was hanging there on the rack when I closed up last night." Then he asked, "Do you suppose it is a ghost?"

Museums house the belongings of people long dead. A shiny badge, an interesting gun, a wanted poster—it's possible that some of these displays of personal items have come with a ghost or two attached. Those who are still not convinced have no explanation as to how and why "Sparky," a toy police car, is moved around late at night when the museum is empty. No matter where the little car is placed, the volunteers know that it will be in a different location every morning. It's the good guys versus the bad guys, even in the afterlife.

Silverland Suites

Cad Thompson stands out, even among the colorful characters who have resided in Virginia City over the years. Thompson, whose real name was Sarah Hagan, came to the Comstock in 1863 with a young son in tow. She took stock of the booming town and quickly set up shop in the red-light district on D Street. The resulting parlor house at Sutton and D Streets became known as the Brick House and was reputed to be one of the finest in Virginia City.

Located near the train depot, the Brick House was a very busy place indeed. Cad enjoyed the profits of her business, but could not endure the harsh Virginia City winters. She often left the Brick in the charge of a younger woman and sojourned in San Francisco. She eventually moved there permanently.

A century later, time has swept away the D Street red-light district. The cribs and the Brick are all long gone. On nearby E Street the Silverland Inn & Suites, Virginia City's newest hotel, has been built. The Silverland's location in the town's former red-light district has led to stories of hauntings. The ghosts are children, some say, but no one is quite sure. Another story has it that this area was once the potters' field, although that is likely untrue.

The Silverland was the site of the 2010 Virginia City Paranormal Conference. During that event, many people reported hearing children running up and down the hallways at all hours of the day and night. No earthly kids were responsible. One conference attendee had a ghostly presence slip into bed with her and another registered some rather naughty EVP during a recording session in her room. The Silverland has also been investigated by some of the local ghost-hunting groups. Their findings bear evidence of a ghostly presence or two.

If you like to sleep where the para-celebs have slept, the Silverland is for you. Nationally known paranormal investigators Zak Bagans, Jason Hawes, Darkness Dave Schrader, Nick Groff, Aaron Goodwin, and Grant Wilson have all spent time here, as has yours truly.

Gold Hill Hotel

Originally known as the Vesey House, Virginia City's Gold Hill Hotel is the oldest continually operating hotel in the state. Built in 1862 during the Comstock's silver boom, the hotel is located near the site of Nevada's worst mining accident. The disaster happened at the Yellow Jacket Mine on the morning of April 6, 1869. A fire broke out eight hundred feet into the mine, leaving the miners trapped by smoke from burning timber and poisonous gasses that spread throughout the tunnels. Rescue attempts were hindered by the flames and smoke; thirty-five men lost their lives in the disaster. Some of the bodies were left where they fell and never recovered.

The ghosts of these miners are said to haunt the Gold Hill Hotel's Miner's Cabin. Since 2007, when it was featured on a popular ghost-hunting TV show, the Miner's Cabin has been regularly booked weeks in advance by ghost investigators. Some of them claim the ghost of a man stays in the cabin's back room. He is filled with negative energy and very angry at someone. Others offer up EVP of harrowing screams. One young couple, after waiting for more than a month to stay in the cabin, packed up and left in the middle of the night. It seems their sleep had been interrupted by the deep, pitiful cries of two ghostly men who kept yanking the covers off their bed.

The ghosts in the main hotel are apparently much happier. Unlike the rustic Miner's Cabin, the main hotel boasts plenty of old world charm. The rooms are elegantly appointed and the fine dining at the Crown Point Restaurant is sure to please. In ghost-hunting circles the main hotel is famous for its two ghosts, those known as William and Rosie.

Both ghosts are said to play pranks. Rosie sometimes shakes the beds of guests. William was blamed for spreading toilet paper across a bathroom one night. William is believed to be a former owner of the hotel who only wants to make sure that his hotel is kept as it should be. He has been known to watch housekeepers as they go about their work. Those who've seen him describe William as tall, dark, mustachioed, and handsome. He likes nothing better than a good cigar, and sometimes chooses to announce his presence with the smell of strong cigar smoke.

Rosie was a young prostitute who died in a terrible buggy accident near the hotel. She took up permanent residence long ago and has no intention of vacating the premises. You'll know she's near when you smell the sweet aroma of heavy lilac perfume. One evening during the Tuesday night lecture series in the hotel's Great Room, the speaker called for Rosie to join the audience. No sooner had she asked for Rosie than the strong aroma of lilac filled the room. If you want to stay in a haunted room, ask for the room of either Rosie or William. But don't say you weren't warned.

Silver Queen Hotel

Imagine that you've come to view the world-famous "Silver Dollar Lady" painting at Virginia City's Silver Queen Hotel. You attempt to count the coins on the lady's dress, and wonder "Is that right?" (For the record, there are 3,261 silver dollars on her dress, and 28 twenty-dollar gold pieces on her belt.) You turn to an elderly man who stands near you. He explains the painting's story and how people from all over the world come to take photographs of the "Silver Dollar Lady."

The old man prattles on about how the Silver Queen was formerly known as the Molinelli Hotel. He seems to be a font of information. So you ask, "What about ghosts? Is this place haunted?"

He looks at you oddly and then disappears. What just happened? Where did the old man go? You ask the bartender. She smiles knowingly. You've just met up with Tiny, the former owner who is still in residence. And just for fun, he likes to share his historical knowledge with tourists.

The Silver Queen Hotel was built in 1876. With twenty-nine rooms, a quaint wedding chapel, and a friendly neighborhood-type bar, the hotel is a Virginia City staple that has been featured on numerous TV shows over the years. And yes, to answer the question, there are several ghosts in residence.

In addition to the prostitute who committed suicide in a bathtub, there is a ghostly young woman who walks through the wall and a ghostly miner who knocks on guests' doors in the middle of the night. The most annoying spirits are the couple in an upstairs room who carry on a long, very loud lover's quarrel. Guests have complained about them for years. Why don't they just kiss and make up?

Strange things happen in the downstairs bar after it is closed for the night and the lights are off. A playful ghost takes over, moving glasses, unplugging lights, and tossing things around with no rhyme or reason. During the early-morning hours, just before the sun comes up over Sugar Loaf, strange shadows play across the windows of the Silver Queen. Some passersby have stopped to see what is going on inside, only to discover the bar is empty. Empty of any living creatures, that is.

Debbie Bender, owner/operator of the Virginia City Ghost Tour, shared the following story: "Although no one has ever seen the cowboy ghost, many people who've stayed at the Silver Queen tell me that they hear his boots on the stairs as he walks up and down. A couple of them have mentioned hearing spurs as well. That's why we call him the Cowboy. But the funny thing about that is . . . take a look. The stairs are carpeted."

Of Ghost Cats and Children

Another story that Debbie Bender shares with her Virginia City Ghost Tour patrons is that of the ghost cat. One night after the walk was concluded, a woman who had just taken the tour pulled Debbie and her partner, Tomas Cruz, aside.

"Why didn't you tell about that ghost cat?" she asked.

Debbie and Tomas looked at each other. Neither of them had heard the story.

Always eager for another story, Debbie asked, "What ghost cat?"

"That cat down by the school. I thought for sure you'd talk about that."

"No." Tomas shook his head. "We haven't heard that one."

"I saw him," said the woman. "He was walking along that alley down there by the school. I called to him and he stopped, almost like he was waiting for me to catch up with him. I was right upon him and bent down to pet him when he ran away, and ran straight through the school's brick wall."

Debbie and Tomas excused themselves, walked down to the middle school, and looked for the cat, to no avail. They've not encountered the ghost kitty. But they have run into other spirits during their tours, including that of a little girl who met a tragic death.

"Do you believe that ghost meters can help with ghost hunting?" Bender asked. "Well let me tell you, it's possible. The little girl who was killed in a carriage accident on C Street is one example. During the tour Tomas and I stop and let people try to communicate with the little girl. She seems to enjoy making the lights [on the meters] blink, stopping and starting.

"One night we had about twenty people on the tour when we stopped at the parking lot in front of Piper's Opera House. The little ghost was having fun turning the meters on and off. Someone suggested we all take a photograph at the same time to see if we could capture any photo evidence. We held our cameras and counted to three. All the flashes went off at the same time. The meters stopped working immediately. I think it might have frightened the little girl. I hope not."

The Cursed Airfield

It's a running joke among ghost hunters about the number of haunted locations that are said to be atop Indian burial grounds. Judging by the mistreatment that many Native Americans were subjected to, it is certainly understandable why this might be. Not all these tales can possibly be true, but in the case of Tonopah's cursed airfield there just might be some truth to the burial ground claims.

Today the Tonopah Air Base stands like a skeleton beneath the harsh Nevada sun. Across the acres of desert sand are sagebrush, countless Joshua trees, and the foundations of long-demolished buildings. Jackrabbits spring into action at the slightest hint of danger. Overhead a hawk swirls on a reconnaissance mission. Owls and rodents have claimed these decaying World War II hangars as their own. Today, with an incessant wind howling through broken window and door frames, it's difficult to imagine that thousands of servicemen and women once lived and worked here. And yet, the airfield is not completely abandoned. It currently serves as Tonopah Municipal Airport, with two runways still in use.

Almost 85 percent of Nevada's land is owned by the federal government. In 1940, with World War II escalating in Europe, Congress realized it was only a matter of time before the United States entered the conflict. Nevada, with its large tracts of empty, federally owned land, was an obvious choice for locating military training facilities and three million acres were annexed in central and southern Nevada for that purpose. When the 1941 attack on Pearl Harbor brought the United States into the war, construction was jump-started at the Tonopah Army Air Field, part of the larger Tonopah Bombing and Gunnery Range, seven miles east of Tonopah. In July 1942 troops began arriving at the airfield. The runways and a few housing units and mess halls were completed at that time. A hospital and barracks would come the following year.

By then World War II was raging. Pilots and crews began training in Bell P-39 Airacobras for overseas combat missions. The official documents tell a grim story of this training. Fifty-nine fatal accidents occurred between 1942 and 1945 at Tonopah Gunnery and Bombing Range and the Tonopah Army Air Field. Of the 257 pilots and crewmembers involved in these accidents, 135 perished.

There were a number of reasons put forth for these deaths: the Bell-39 Airacobras were old and not maintained well, the pilots and flight crews were inexperienced, and the base was located at high altitudes. But there were also freak accidents. A B-24 crewmember was killed instantly when he walked into a spinning propeller blade. Two men suffocated to death in gun turrets when their oxygen supply was interrupted. Three officers perished in a fire that raged through the barracks. Strangest of all was a machine gun that went out of control, firing in all directions and killing three men.

All these incidents led to whispers of the air base being cursed. No one wanted to serve in Tonopah. A song was even written about the Tonopah Air Field and how bad it was. In the middle of the desert, with the nearest (very small) town seven miles distant, servicemen and women felt keenly isolated. There were just too many crashes and accidents. Was low morale, the terrain, the high altitude, or tired or inexperienced crews to blame? Whatever the reason, it was eventually determined that this was not the place to successfully train fighter pilots, so the operation was changed to a high-altitude training base for B-24 Liberator bomber crews. By the time the base was placed on inactive status in 1945, a new commanding officer, Col. John Faegin, had been assigned here and the safety record had been improved.

Allen Metscher, a Goldfield and Tonopah historian and co-founder of the Central Nevada Museum, has made it his goal to see that the men who died at the Tonopah Air Field are not forgotten. He has spent decades sifting through the remote area that surrounds the airfield in search of relics from the era. In those years he has discovered many things, including rusted plane parts and small human bone fragments. With the information he gleaned, Metscher has created a memorial display at the museum and helped bring closure to the families of the dead. He doesn't believe in ghosts but he understands that some considered the airfield to be jinxed.

During a tour of the base in which a group of ghost hunters took part, Metscher led them into the old hangar. As ghost hunters pulled out their video cameras and audio recorders, he explained how Chuck Yeager supposedly flew his plane through the open doors of the hangar.

Ghosts were forgotten the moment two owls were discovered high up in the rafters. As the ghost hunters pointed their cameras at the owls, those who wanted EVP walked in another direction. With the wind whipping through the hangar, EVP was going to be difficult to capture. And yet, a woman later realized that she had music playing on her recorder. When asked about this the following day, Metscher said that yes, big bands had entertained service people in that particular hangar. Interesting, certainly, but not as much as the ghostly pilot someone saw in another hangar. She turned to ask others if they were seeing him as well. When she turned back, the hangar was empty.

And so it is at the cursed airfield. Between the eerie silence and the howling winds, the sounds of raucous laughter and panicked screaming can sometimes be heard among the ruins of the buildings. Skeptics claim these anomalous sounds are nothing but the wind. Others aren't so sure.

The Mizpah Hotel

When the Mizpah Hotel was built near the Mizpah Mine entrance in 1908, Tonopah was a thriving community, much like Goldfield some twenty-seven miles to the south. At the time, silver and gold discoveries were creating unbelievable wealth. Tonopah and Goldfield, in the heart of the boom area, drew the state's movers and shakers.

The Mizpah Hotel opened with a gala celebration on November 17, 1908, and was meant to accommodate the powerful and their cronies. These were people like Nevada's most powerful man,

George Wingfield, who had a financial connection to both the Mizpah and the Goldfield Hotel. The two hotels were designed by the Reno architectural firm of Holesworth and Curtis. The Goldfield Hotel was the larger of the two, but Mizpah was one floor taller. The five-story structure would rank as Nevada's tallest building until Reno's Mapes Hotel was built after World War II.

When the mines went bust, so did the boomtowns that had grown up around them. The Goldfield Hotel closed after World War II, never to reopen, and Goldfield would all but become a ghost town. Tonopah would see one business after another close. The once-grand Mizpah Hotel changed hands numerous times, and was always financially shaky. It was during its many closures and reopenings that the legends began.

In 1957 eccentric millionaire Howard Hughes married actress Jean Peters at the Mizpah Hotel, or so the story goes. The lovebirds did wed in Tonopah, but the secret ceremony took place nowhere near the hotel. Then there is the legend of United States senator Key Pittman. The senator was rumored to have died days before the 1940 election. It was said that Democratic Party supporters kept his death a secret and stored his body on ice in one of the Mizpah Hotel's clawfoot bathtubs so that Pittman could remain on the ballot and the party could retain the seat. Once Pittman's victory was secure, it was announced that the senator had passed away. Nevada state archivist Guy Rocha has dispelled the tale as untrue a dozen times—Pittman actually died five days after the election, and his fatal heart attack occurred at the Riverside Hotel in Reno, not at the Mizpah. Despite that evidence, there have been numerous sightings of Pittman alleged by people who haven't heard the story and don't have a clue who he was.

The most famous ghost at the Mizpah is the "Lady in Red." A beautiful young prostitute from the Roaring Twenties who crossed her lover one too many times, she paid with her life. There is some confusion has to how she met her death. According to some, the lady was stabbed. As proof of their theory, they say that bloodstains occasionally appear on the exact spot of her demise. Others believe she was strangled. Either way, the Lady in Red is dead. She walks the halls of the fifth floor, where she was murdered, and is known to follow people into the elevator and into their rooms.

Since the hotel's grand reopening in August 2011, people have collected EVP and reported ghostly experiences throughout the hotel. Cold spots, disembodied voices, and sightings of the Lady in Red are the most common. Entertainer Robert Allen stayed in the "Lady in Red Room" on the fifth floor and could not believe his eyes when the dresser drawer opened and closed of its own accord. He did not see the Lady, but he knew she was near. She is also not alone. Patrons occasionally encounter a grizzled old man stomping through the hallways. He's the ghost of an old miner who died in the nearby Mizpah Mine. He sometimes makes an appearance in the elevator. Don't bother asking him what floor he wants. He'll be leaving the elevator sometime before it stops.

Rhyolite

Nevada's landscape is dotted with the remnants of boom-and-bust towns, settlements that rose up almost overnight following a rich ore discovery. But when the mines stopped producing, those who'd come with the idea of striking it rich packed up and moved on, leaving the towns to wither away and die. Rhyolite, near the small town of Beatty and the entrance to Death Valley National Park, was just such a place. On a sweltering summer day in August 1904, gold was discovered nearby. When the news leaked, the desolate area was soon swarming with men and women hoping to strike it rich.

Tents were pitched in every direction, claims were staked, and people kept coming. Two years after the first discovery, Rhyolite began to build toward permanency—the town of three thousand citizens would boast a bank, a railroad station, three railroad lines, two hospitals, schools, churches, more than a dozen grocery stores, and numerous saloons.

By 1912 the boom was over. There wasn't enough gold to sustain mining operations. Most of those who had come to Rhyolite would go elsewhere, leaving the town to crumble in the desert sun. Only the ghostly residents stayed behind. Tom Kelly, who built the famous "Bottle House" in 1906 using thirty thousand bottles, is among the ghosts one might encounter while exploring the ruins of Rhyolite. If you hear an unexplained sound, it could be the ghost of an old town drunk still singing happily. He occasionally serenades tourists, but by all accounts he can't carry a tune.

Like all Old West towns, Rhyolite had a red-light district. At least one of the ladies has stayed on. A ghostly prostitute named Isabella Haskins is the apparition most often spotted. Isabella has been mistaken for a real person more than once as she dashes among the sagebrush. Isabella's gravesite near the site of the old jail is easy to find. Just look for all the glittery baubles and other colorful items that are left in remembrance of how unfairly she was treated after her death. Because she was a lady of the evening, Isabella could not be buried among Rhyolite's other dead. She rests in the only place considered suitable—near the jail. The ghost of a long-dead bad man is also said to walk the decaying buildings day and night. Like Isabella, he is sometimes mistaken for a real person.

Over the years several films have been shot in and around Rhyolite, including the 1925 silent film *The Air Mail* and the 1987 cult classic *Cherry 2000*. The U.S. Bureau of Land Management now oversees Rhyolite, which is one of Nevada's most-photographed locations. There is no better place to stargaze than out here in the desert. While you're in Rhyolite, stop in at the adjacent Goldwell Open Air Museum and Artist Residency. This unique and picturesque place is not to be missed. Please be careful while you're exploring, as ghosts aren't the only residents of the area. Rattlesnakes, and lots of them, are here as well.

Las Vegas

LAS VEGAS WAS FOUNDED IN 1855 AS A MORMON SETTLEMENT. FIFTY years later it had developed into a railroad town. In the last few decades the city has become a metropolis with more than a million residents. Las Vegas is the jewel of the desert and the city that never sleeps. With its glamorous hotel-casino resorts, sunny desert climate, and non-stop entertainment, Las Vegas has become a favorite destination of tourists from all over the world. Some have never left, even in death.

Tupac Shakur

Grammy-nominated rap artist and burgeoning actor Tupac Shakur was gunned down in Las Vegas on September 7, 1996. Shakur's killing occurred as Tupac rode shotgun while his friend Suge Knight was at the wheel of a shiny new BMW. Earlier that night Shakur and Knight had been ringside when Mike Tyson knocked out Bruce Seldon in a disappointingly short 103-second boxing match. The rapper had decided against wearing his bulletproof vest that night, an accessory deemed necessary after he was wounded in a shooting in October 1995.

As Knight's BMW rolled up to the intersection of Koval and Flamingo, a white Cadillac pulled up alongside at the light. Without a word the Caddy's occupants opened fire, pumping five bullets into the BMW and mortally wounding Shakur. Six days later, on Friday the 13th, Shakur died of his injuries at the Southern Nevada University Medical Center. Although there were a number of names put forth as suspects, no one has been charged with his murder.

There are those who believe Shakur's death is one big hoax. Much like the theories surrounding the death of Elvis Presley, some believe Tupac Shakur faked his own death and is living it up at some unknown location. Why either man would do such a thing is never fully explained. There is evidence refuting the hoax claims. In Shakur's case there is the grisly autopsy photo that made its way into the public years ago. And let's not forget the many sightings of a ghostly Tupac in the area of Koval and Flamingo since his Friday the 13th death.

Paranormal researchers know that a ghost often stays at the location where he or she met death, especially if that death was violent and unexpected. A psychic has put forth the theory that Shakur is seeking justice and attempting to solve his own murder. Another believes he liked Las Vegas and simply doesn't want to leave.

Redd Foxx

Redd Foxx's death from a massive heart attack on October 11, 1991, cut short the actor's desperately needed comeback. At the time of his death, Foxx had been attempting a return to television by co-starring with his friend Della Reese in a new series titled *The Royal Family*.

Born John Elroy Sanford, his long career as a successful lounge comedian began at a time when racism ran rampant in Las Vegas. But Foxx succeeded, and this gave him entrée into weekly television and subsequent stardom. From 1972 to 1977 his salary for playing Fred Sanford on the wildly popular series *Sanford and Son* paid the bills. And the living was strictly Las Vegas lavish. Foxx lived large in a mansion on Eastern Avenue, complete with the ubiquitous swimming pool, several cars, fancy clothes, and all the trappings of wealth. He also liked to play Keno at the local hotel-casinos. When the show ended in 1977, so did the big paychecks. But the demands of the Internal Revenue Service did not.

Redd ignored them, reasoning that he wasn't that wealthy and that he didn't owe that much. He found out the hard way there is no escaping income tax. After tax liens were placed against him the entertainer was stunned to find IRS agents on the doorstep of his home at 5460 S. Eastern Avenue. His house and other assets were seized to cover his tax bill. Redd Foxx left his home with the clothes on his back and little else. Subsequently, his mansion was prepared for sale.

Foxx was on his way back up the financial ladder when the fatal heart attack struck. And as every ghost hunter knows, there is nothing like unfinished business to keep a ghost haunting a location. So it was at Redd Foxx's place. Eventually the mansion was put up for auction and sold to a fan of Redd's. This was a man that didn't believe in ghosts and hauntings, at least not until things started happening. Unexplained noises at all hours, floors creaking as if someone were walking across them, and sliding glass doors that slammed opened and shut all helped convince him to seek the help of a psychic.

It was determined that Redd Foxx was still very angry at the IRS. Although they had chased him from his home when he was alive, they could not do so now that he was dead. Redd was not ready to vacate the premises. However, the new buyer was. The house was next sold to a vacuum cleaner business. The company moved in after a quick remodel and conversion to offices. Employees immediately had problems with their computers and their desks. Those who went out for lunch sometimes returned to find papers strewn everywhere.

One employee claimed to have witnessed Redd Foxx's apparition walk across the room as she was working late one night. Neighbors complained about the noise from a loud and sordid spousal argument between Redd and one of his wives near the swimming pool. No one was anywhere near the pool, and hadn't been in quite a long time. The ghost stories were a form of free advertisement, but not the sort the vacuum cleaner company wanted. They moved out.

Ghost hunters came and did their investigations. Some of them felt that Redd had moved on. Others disagreed. They felt he was still in the house and would leave in good time. The house was once again renovated and the swimming pool was filled in and paved over to create a parking lot. Shannon Day Realty moved into Foxx's former house. As a concession to Redd a little red fox was painted onto the sign in front of the property. Apparently this made Foxx happy; for the time being, the ghostly activity has stopped.

The Luxor

The sphinx and pyramid of the Luxor Hotel Casino is the first sight seen by some airline passengers arriving at McCarran International Airport. Shimmering in the hot desert sun, the pyramid has become as much a part of the city's aura as Sunrise Mountain and gambling chips. The 4,407-room hotel was uniquely designed to afford guests who step into the hallways a breathtaking view of the main floor below. The Luxor is also known for its "Sky Beam," the vertical shaft of light shining from atop the pyramid. Hotel operators once claimed it was the world's most powerful beam of light; it can be seen by airline pilots hundreds of miles distant and by astronauts circling Earth. Hundreds of bats swarm around the light nightly in search of bugs to eat.

One superstition holds that the placement of the sphinx is wrong. Rather than facing eastward, as it currently does, some believe the sphinx should be facing the setting sun. Because of this oversight, the city has been cursed. Or at least it will have a heap of bad luck to contend with.

Long before groundbreaking began on the Luxor in 1993, locals say this location was a favorite dumping ground for the bodies of noncompliant mobsters. This might explain the ghost of a man in a brown striped suit. Brown suits haven't been all that popular since mobsters ruled Vegas. The ghost is said to be middle-aged and harried. Perhaps he had an inkling that his time was up.

The brown-suited mobster's death may have been murder, but other Luxor ghosts were victims of different fates. One is the ghost of a worker who died in an accident during construction of the fabulous hotel-casino. This death and the many accidents that were befalling the location increased whispers that the Luxor was cursed. Several superstitious people refused to work at the site. Despite that, work continued and the Luxor opened in 1993.

The hotel had only recently opened when an elegantly attired young woman walked across the casino floor and made her way to the inclinator (the Luxor's term for its elevators), which she took to the twenty-sixth floor. She stepped out of the inclinator and for a brief moment stood near the railing, looking down at the action below. She then climbed over the railing and leapt to her death, landing in the ground-floor casino. Her apparition is usually spotted walking aimlessly in the casino area.

History and movie buffs have a thrill in store for them at the Luxor's Titanic Artifact Exhibit. Featuring many relics from the disaster, including passenger's papers and gaming chips, the exhibit offers a rare glimpse of what it was like on the grand ship. Those who practice psychometry, the ability to know things about a person by touching his or her personal belongings, may discover more. Who's to say a ghost or two didn't come along with the artifacts?

The Flamingo

How many cities pay homage to a mobster with a memorial, such as that for Benjamin "Bugsy" Siegel at the Flamingo? It is apparently not the only reminder of Siegel at the venerable casino: ever since his June 1947 murder there have been sightings of Bugsy's smiling phantom here. He is nattily attired in a smoking jacket and slacks in the style of times past. He usually appears in and around the resort's rose garden and wedding chapel.

Bugsy, some say, is the true father of Las Vegas. After all, it was his foresight that started it all when he led his gangster pals to the Nevada desert in the first place. In appreciation of his initiative, the debonair mobster was left in charge of construction of the Flamingo.

Overseeing it all proved too much of a temptation for Bugsy. He may have had the vision to see Las Vegas's potential, but it was rumored that he just couldn't keep his hands off his bosses' money. By the time they wised up, he'd managed to steal a bundle from them. This could be one of the reasons he was murdered while reading the Sunday newspaper in the swank Beverly Hills home of his girlfriend, Virginia Hill.

Before it was razed in 1993, Bugsy's old suite at the Flamingo was the site of paranormal activity. It has always been assumed that Bugsy Siegel was the ghost responsible for the strange occurrences. But was he? Paranormal researchers try to find explanations for ghosts and hauntings. It was discovered there might be another possibility for the weirdness that went on in Bugsy's suite.

On September 15, 1952, a murder-suicide took place at the Flamingo Hotel in Siegel's former penthouse suite. Nineteen-year-old Adrian Grodnick turned his gun on himself after killing his fiancée, Betty Baron.

Several hours later two housekeepers knocked on the door. When they received no answer, they knocked again and again. Finally they forced their way into the suite through the locked door. Sprawled across the bed were the nude bodies of Grodnick and Baron. Grodnick was the son of a wealthy New York businessman. Baron was a recent graduate of UCLA. According to her family, the pair met and fell in love when Grodnick moved into the Los Angeles apartment building her parents managed. Baron, at twenty-six, was several years older than Grodnick.

Marriage plans ensued. It was to be a big church wedding with all the trappings: flowers, white gown, half-carat sparkler, tiered cake, and tuxedo. Grodnick, who was soon to be inducted into the army, wanted things simpler. So he rented a car and took Betty to Las Vegas to get married in a quickie Nevada-style wedding. They could then return to L.A. and do the big wedding, with no one the wiser.

Betty agreed. They checked into the $35-a-night penthouse at the Flamingo and spent their time on typical Vegas pursuits: gambling, drinking, and floorshows by night, and sunbathing poolside by day. During those two days something went wrong. For whatever reasons, Adrian sneaked away to a pawnshop and bought a gun. Later, investigators would theorize he was so frightened of his impending military service that he killed Betty and himself.

Another theory put forth had Grodnick apprehensive about Betty's faithfulness while he was stationed overseas. Maybe he was insanely jealous. Perhaps there were accusations, tears, and threats to end the romance. For whatever reason, Betty Baron was shot twice in the head while she slept by the man she loved and trusted.

Grodnick then put the revolver to his own head and pulled the trigger. Perhaps they, not the infamous Bugsy Siegel, were the ones haunting the suite all those years.

Bally's

The MGM Grand Hotel fire on November 21, 1980, is the deadliest disaster in Nevada's history. The magnificent Bally's hotel-casino now stands on the spot where this tragedy took place. The tower in which so many people lost their lives is still in use today. Some believe the property is haunted because of this tragic event. Others insist that the stories of ghostly weeping and disoriented apparitions are nothing but the products of overworked imaginations.

Upon its completion in 1973, the towering twenty-six-story MGM Grand was one of the newest and most elegant hotel-casinos in Las Vegas, a new standard by which others would be compared. The sawdust floors of early Las Vegas were long gone, replaced by the MGM Grand's lavish nine-hundred-seat showroom and shimmering cut-glass chandeliers.

On November 21, 1980, Comdek, the electronic convention, was in town. Business was booming throughout Vegas and the MGM Grand's rooms were almost completely booked. Early in the morning an electrical ground-fault wire sparked, causing a fire to break out in the MGM Grand's Deli Restaurant. Employees were unable to contain the blaze, which soon flashed out of control. Without sprinklers to slow the fire's progress, the flames rapidly swept into the casino level, melting plastic interiors and emitting noxious, lethal fumes. Of the five thousand people who were in the hotel when the fire broke out, eighty-five died, most of them from smoke inhalation. Some of those trapped in the upper floors leaped to their deaths rather than die in the flames. Seven hundred others were injured but escaped with their lives.

Lawsuits—1,357 of them—were filed against 118 companies, and a settlement of $223 million was reached. Within eight months the fire-damaged hotel-casino was repaired and re-opened under the Bally's name. The MGM built a new hotel-casino a few blocks away. New and improved fire safety codes and retrofits were enacted as a result of the tragic MGM Grand fire. Today at the site it's business as usual . . . except for the ghosts.

The sounds of disembodied weeping and coughing have been heard in a seventh-floor hallway more than once. Some guests have reported the apparition of a man who seems to be lost, running aimlessly through the same hallway, only to vanish into a wall. There are also said to be ghostly gamblers in the same casino area where people died as they sat dropping coins into the slot machines.

The Bellagio

Calling itself the "Miracle in the Desert," the Dunes hotel-casino opened on the Strip in May 1955. Showbiz hotshots of the time like Jayne Mansfield, Liberace, Judy Garland, and Frank Sinatra were eager to perform at the biggest place on the Strip.

Back in that day, it was common knowledge that the Mob ruled Las Vegas. Mafia money built and controlled the Dunes; it was this same ill-gotten gain that helped to keep the hotel-casino afloat. But competition was stiff. The Dunes faced one financial crisis after another until management decided to try something different. That "something different" was Minsky's Follies, which opened in 1957 in the Aladdin Room. It was the first topless show ever held in a Las Vegas hotel-casino and it was a major success. Up in Carson City, the state legislature was scandalized, but the audiences told the story. A record-breaking sixteen thousand people came that first week to see the show. There would be no going back for the Dunes or for Las Vegas.

Once out of the red, the Dunes expanded. A new golf course and a convention center were built, followed in 1961 by the twenty-four-story Dunes Tower.

But times change, and the Dunes lost its glitter. Larger, more lavish, and more modern hotel-casinos were being built. New owners tried, but no one could save the sinking Dunes. Casino magnate Steve Wynn ponied up seventy-five million dollars and the Dunes was his. The old hotel-casino was doomed. Wynn wanted the property, not the dinky, outdated buildings. In true Las Vegas style, the Dunes was brought down in a most spectacular fashion. On the night of October 27, 1993, the Dunes was imploded in a fireworks extravaganza witnessed by more than two hundred thousand people. Old Las Vegas was dead.

Within a year the posh Bellagio was built on the same site and the Dunes faded into the past, just a memory. But are there more than just memories left? Cold spots, which are good indicators of something paranormal, have been reported numerous times in the Bellagio. A glowing blue figure appears out of nowhere and vanishes into nothingness at places throughout the hotel. He may be a low-ranking mobster who displeased his bosses. Or he may be something else: in ghost theory it is believed that rather than staying at the scene of one's death or final resting spot, a person may return to a favorite location. The glowing blue figure could just as easily be someone from Milwaukee who vacationed in Vegas regularly in life. And after death he has decided to extend that vacation indefinitely.

The Oasis Motel

Some places seem to draw the world-weary. Such is the Oasis Motel, located at 1731 Las Vegas Boulevard South, the end of the Strip. This area is not featured in the slick tourist leaflets found all over town, but several ghost-hunting groups have investigated the motel. Some have collected evidence such as EVP and photographs of ghosts. Television ghost-hunting star Zak Bagans claims to have had a real-time, two-way conversation with deceased actor David Strickland during an EVP session at the Oasis. The ghosts of the Oasis may soon have fewer people to communicate with. The city recently shut the Oasis down for prostitution and code and licensing violations. At the time of this writing it is closed indefinitely.

Stu Ungar was the first celebrity to die at the motel. Flush with newly won cash, the poker pro paid for two nights in advance and checked into Room 6 of the Oasis on November 20, 1998. It was after 11:00 A.M. when motel employees knocked on his door. Receiving no answer, they unlocked the door and discovered Ungar had already checked out of the land of the living.

A known drug user, Ungar still had hundreds of dollars in cash on him. Police searched the room but found no drug paraphernalia. The death wasn't a homicide and didn't appear to be a suicide. Later autopsy findings indicated the forty-five-year-old Ungar had died of a heart condition brought on by years of drug abuse. The man who had won millions at poker was dead. His friends took up a collection so that he would have a funeral and a final resting place at Palm Valley View Memorial Park in East Las Vegas.

Four months after Ungar's death, actor David Strickland checked into the Oasis. Strickland, who played Todd on the popular Brooke Shields television series *Suddenly Susan*, could have afforded a better, swankier room on the Strip. Instead he chose the Oasis. After spending several hours partying at a strip club with friend and fellow actor Andy Dick, Strickland went back to Room 20 at the Oasis.

After downing a six-pack, Strickland pulled a sheet off the bed, wrapped it around a ceiling beam, and hanged himself. A maid discovered him when she walked into the room later that morning. Whether it was a spur-of-the-moment decision or one he had planned for some time, we will never know. He left no suicide note behind. The actor was scheduled to appear in court that day in Los Angeles on a drug charge. Perhaps he saw his career crumbling under the weight of drug abuse.

Since that time, the Oasis drawn paranormal investigators. Visitors have reported hearing strange noises and experiencing feelings of panic, leading some to believe the tragic figures of the Oasis have never really checked out.

When in Doubt, Blame a Ghost

Las Vegas is a city that lives on chance. Double down or stay? Walk away or let it ride? Certainly Samuel Marquez's victim, Richard Adamicki, was unlucky for ever having crossed paths with him, and for ever having shown kindness toward him. In repayment for the bartender's kindness, Marquez battered Adamicki over the head with a baseball bat, robbed him, and left him to die. Unfortunately for Marquez his crime was caught on tape. Marquez confessed and was given a one-hundred-year sentence. That might have been the end of it. Except Marquez had a ghost story to tell—and tell it he did, all the way to the Nevada Supreme Court.

Marquez claimed he saw the ghost of a woman who demanded that he rob and kill, which he argued proved that he was legally insane. Marquez claimed to have had encounters with the ghost since childhood and may have even been afraid the specter was there to take him on to the afterlife. No one bought it. In the Silver State one must be delusional and unable to distinguish right from wrong in order to be declared legally insane.

So did Marquez know that killing Adamicki was wrong? That was the question that propelled the case all the way to the Nevada Supreme Court. In a 2-1 decision, the court decided Marquez was not insane when he beat Adamicki. The sentence would continue, and it was back to prison for Marquez.

Goodsprings Pioneer Saloon

Goodsprings is only about forty miles southwest of Las Vegas, but the tiny town is a world apart. There are no neon signs, traffic jams, or crowds here. In 1914 this area was rich in zinc and copper. World War I caused the prices of these metals to skyrocket, which brought an influx of money, businesses, and people to Goodsprings. At one time there were more than thirty mines operating in the area.

Nowadays the town is relatively quiet. Over in the old cemetery a couple of ghostly children are said to roam at night. Ghost-hunting groups have done several investigations there, but the two little specters have not been positively identified. Among the town's buildings, the Pioneer Saloon, built in 1913, is a favorite with ghost hunters and happens to be the locals' hangout as well. Friendly barkeeps and Old West-style décor lend the saloon an aura of down-home fun.

The saloon is said to be haunted by the ghost of one Paul Coski, a card-playing gambler whose cheating ways eventually spelled his doom. Shot dead at the poker table, the bewhiskered gambler roams the premises still. Bullet holes in the tin ceiling are thought to be remnants of that shooting. Coski's apparition is usually spotted at the front door or sitting at the end of the bar.

Some claim the ghost of actress Carol Lombard parties at the Pioneer Saloon along with the love of her life (and afterlife), Clark Gable. Lombard was killed in 1942 when her plane slammed into nearby Mount Potosi, killing all on board. Gable spent many anxious hours awaiting word of survivors at the El Rancho Vegas in

Las Vegas and the Fayle Hotel and the Pioneer Saloon in Good-springs. The saloon's employees can show you the spot on the bar where Gable's cigarettes burned deep into the wood. A display in the pool room honors Lombard and Gable.

Regular ghost hunts at the Pioneer have turned up a wealth of evidence that the saloon is indeed haunted. Aside from the usual cold spots and photos of ghostly manifestations, some of those taking part in the investigations have reported being touched or hearing their name whispered. Psychic-medium Deborah Carr Senger visited the saloon several years ago with friends. This is what she had to say about that afternoon:

> As we drove up I noticed this blonde bombshell standing off to the right of the front door. She was smiling broadly and I wondered what she was doing there, dressed in such an elegant evening gown at this time of day. My friends and I went inside and I didn't give her another thought. We sat at the bar and I excused myself and went to ladies' room. There was a young girl inside crying. "Excuse me," I said and started to step back out, when I suddenly realized that she was a ghost. "What is the matter? Why are you crying?" I asked.
>
> "Will you find my mom and tell her that I'm okay? It's good over here."
>
> "I can try," I said. "But what's your name?"
>
> "Sarah," she cried. "Please . . . oh please . . . tell my mom that I'm okay."
>
> Promising to try, I left the bathroom and hurried back to the bar.
>
> "You're not going to believe what just happened in there," I told my friends.
>
> The bartender stopped wiping down the bar. "I would," she laughed.
>
> "Oh?"
>
> "You've met Sarah. And she wants you to tell her mother she is happy."
>
> "But who was she? Where is her mother?"
>
> "No one knows," the bartender said, moving down the bar. "But all the same, good luck finding her."
>
> The whole thing left me unsettled. It's bad enough to find live people in trouble, but when you encounter a person who is dead and wanting help, that's heartbreaking, especially when you can't

do anything for them. To take my mind off the ghost crying in the bathroom, my friends suggested we go into the pool room and look around. I looked at the pool table, then at the walls. And there was the blonde bombshell from out front, Carol Lombard! The same Carol Lombard that died in the airplane crash nearby.

Robert George Allen, owner of the Goodsprings Ghost Hunt, was recently conducting a tour at the saloon. During a session with a spirit box (a piece of ghost-hunting equipment said to make communication with spirits possible), Allen asked if anyone was there.

"Clark Gable," came the reply.

"Who are you?" Robert asked.

"Clark Gable."

"Okay," Robert said. "If there is anyone else here, what's your name?"

"Jane," a woman's voice answered. Jane was Carol Lombard's given name.

Besides Lombard, twenty-one others were aboard the TWA plane when it slammed into Mount Potosi en route from Las Vegas to Los Angeles. The rescue effort was hampered by the remote crash location and inclement weather. It was mid-January and snow was already heavy in the higher elevations. From a makeshift operations headquarters in Goodsprings, searchers hiked up the side of the mountain toward the crash site. Theirs, they soon discovered, was not to be a rescue mission.

Charred and broken bodies were strewn around the wreckage. One person would later say that the snow was red with blood. Lombard's burned body was discovered under one of the wings. It would take dental charts flown in from Hollywood to positively identify the blonde comedian.

As the bodies were recovered, they were wrapped in brown army blankets, carefully hoisted down the cliff, and taken by horse to Goodsprings. Army ambulances transported them to Las Vegas.

By all accounts Carole Lombard loved to party and have a good time. Perhaps she still does here at the Pioneer Saloon. There have been encounters with an apparition believed to be her. And why not? Stars love the camera and attention.

Hoover Dam

Hoover Dam has been rumored to host its share of ghostly activity since its completion in 1935. Stories of hauntings abound, but the tales that involve the bodies of workers being buried within the dam's concrete walls may be the strangest of all—and are not true.

Work on the dam was dangerous. The desert heat was unbearable. While there is some disagreement as to how many people died while working on the project, ninety-six is the officially recognized number. All of the bodies were quickly recovered.

Although there is no truth to the tales of bodies buried in the concrete, this doesn't mean that the dam doesn't have its ghosts. The phantom of a worker is probably the best-known spirit. He is believed to be a young man who died while working the night shift long ago. The ghostly man usually appears in hard hat and work clothes, ready to resume his duties. He has been spotted near the elevator and at certain workstations near the generators.

The construction of Hoover Dam and the creation of Lake Mead also disturbed the dead, which is always considered a risky proposition. As the Colorado River rushed in to fill the new reservoir, three small towns—St. Thomas, Rioville, and Callville—were submerged. Their residents had already packed up and moved on by that time. Most relocated to nearby Overton. None of them had wanted to leave their dead in cemeteries beneath Lake Mead, so they had taken the bodies with them; graves were dug up and the dead reburied in a cemetery in Overton.

Along Highway 50, America's Loneliest Road

U.S. HIGHWAY 50 FOLLOWS THE OLD TRAIL ACROSS NORTHERN NEVADA once used by Pony Express riders in the state's early days. In 1986 *Life* magazine dubbed Nevada's 287-mile stretch of Highway 50 "the Loneliest Road in America," and for good reason. Motorists weren't likely to see much traffic on this road. Today, it's still possible to travel endless miles along this stretch before coming across another vehicle, much less a town. You may come across some ghosts, though.

Lander County Courthouse

Austin is one of the tiny towns scattered along Highway 50. Situated on the sides of Pony Canyon and named after the city in Texas, Austin was home to nearly ten thousand people in its heyday. Now fewer than five hundred folks call the town home.

Anyone who enjoys strolling through old graveyards will find Austin's cemetery fascinating. It comprises five cemeteries located on either side of Highway 50, with the oldest section on the west side of the highway. First used for burials in the early 1860s, the cemetery offers a spectacular view of nearby mountains. Also of note are its two angel headstones, rarities in old Nevada cemeteries.

There certainly was enough death in early Austin to fill those cemeteries. Three years before the Lander County Courthouse was built in Austin, twenty-year-old Rufus B. Anderson was hanged on October 30, 1868, in what newspapers called "another civilizing gallows scene." In reality, Anderson's execution was anything but civilized.

Five months earlier, Anderson had shot and killed Noble T. Slocum. He was brought to trial, found guilty, and condemned to die for his crime. But Anderson proved to be a man the state of Nevada couldn't easily hang. After a lengthy legal battle that went all the way to the Nevada Supreme Court, a date was set for Anderson's execution. His would not be a swift death. The first attempt to hang him met with failure when the knot broke. The executioner quickly slipped the noose back around Anderson's neck and for the second time Anderson prepared to meet his maker. But something went wrong again. Anderson dropped to the ground with a thud. The crowd of spectators became unruly; Anderson had defied death twice, which they took as a sign. They demanded that the execution be stopped. They rushed up to free the condemned man, but militia guards stepped in. Justice was not to be denied.

A chair was brought to the gallows and Anderson sat on it a moment. For the third and final time a noose was slipped around his neck. This time the hanging was successful and Anderson was quickly hoisted into the hereafter.

In 1871, with Austin's population growing, a fine two-story brick courthouse was built to replace the small wooden structure that had previously been used. Ten years later, on a cold December night in 1881, vigilantes rushed the jail on the ground floor of the building. Seething with rage and bent on justice, the mob pulled Richard Jennings from his jail cell and up the stairs to the balcony. The previous night Jennings had shot and killed John A. Barrett, a well-liked rancher, without provocation. Now he was about to be lynched.

But before he was strung up, Jennings had something to say, and according to the *Reese River Reveille*, he agreed with his executioners. "Oh my Boys, I guess I deserve this," he said. The newspaper also warned would-be bad guys to stay away, unless they wanted to meet the same fate as Jennings.

The courthouse hasn't been used for trials since 1979, when voters approved the relocation of the county seat from Austin to Battle Mountain. County commissioners then moved their offices into the old courthouse. They are sharing the building with a ghost who is said to noisily walk up and down the stairs, fill the room with a cold chill, and open and shut doors loudly. A former employee of the building told of having her pencils and notes continually misplaced. At first she thought it was her own forgetfulness. But she soon realized that there was something more going on. There was no other explanation for why her office supplies moved from one area of her office to the next in a matter of seconds. She concluded that it was the work of a ghost.

So who is the ghost that makes a nuisance of himself in the old courthouse? Because justice was denied him, Jennings is a possible candidate. But it could also be Rufus B. Anderson, who surely was angry at the way his execution was botched.

International Hotel

Lumber was a precious commodity in Nevada's early days. When one place was done with it, chances were the lumber could be used elsewhere. So it was that Austin's International Hotel was built of lumber that was hauled across the desert from Virginia City in 1863. The International Hotel has long since stopped booking guests. But locals and those just passing through can still enjoy the International's bar and restaurant. Friendly as the folks might be in Austin, the ghost who resides here is not the social type; he prefers to keep to himself. Regulars call their ghost "Tommy." Anyone that scoffs and openly denies his existence just might make his angry acquaintance. Years ago a customer at the bar found this out the hard way. After loudly stating that ghosts were nothing but the products of overworked imaginations, the man was startled by an icy chill of cold air blowing down the back of his neck.

Some are certain that the ghost is that of a regular guest who died in the hotel long ago. But the ghost could just as easily be a resident spirit that came along for the ride when all that lumber was being hauled in from Virginia City.

Eureka Opera House

In its heyday, Eureka was Nevada's second-largest city and just as wild as any other Western town. With its rich and colorful history, the small town on the Loneliest Road in America has much to offer visitors. The Eureka Opera House is one of many places of interest here, and is also available for special events such as weddings and parties.

A photographers' favorite, the Eureka Opera House is only one of two restored and usable opera houses in the state of Nevada; Piper's Opera House in Virginia City is the other (see page 70). The Eureka Opera House was built at this location after an 1879 fire destroyed the old Odd Fellows Building that once stood here. The opera house was not only used for live performances, but also for showing silent films and movies. It eventually fell into disrepair and was closed in the 1950s.

The opera house has since been renovated and is believed to be haunted. People here take reports of cold breezes and the disembodied voices in stride. Whoever the resident wraith is, he or she means no harm, and is most likely just a frustrated actor seeking the limelight. Of course there is also the possibility that this ghost was a victim of the fire that destroyed the original building here, and has decided to stick around on this earthly plane for awhile.

The Jackson House

The Jackson House was built in Eureka in 1877, at a time when travel from one side of the state to the other took days. It was to be an elegant respite for travelers weary from the long journey across Nevada's desert. Apparently some of those travelers liked the hotel's ambiance so much they decided to stay on indefinitely. The hotel offers nineteen rooms, a restaurant, a bar, and those aforementioned ghosts. Three ghostly children and a woman who is most likely their mother or governess have taken up residence at the Jackson House.

The apparitions very rarely make an appearance. When they do, it is either on the stairs or in the hallway. Those who've seen them say their attire is that of the late nineteenth century. At times the heedless youngsters are boisterous. Over the years, guests have told of hearing them scamper through the building or giggle in the shadows. Even though the phantom woman does her best to keep an eye on them, the ghostly children are never well behaved. No doubt, she is the indulgent sort and very seldom reprimands them.

The Ghost of Kate Miller

Kate Miller died in a barroom brawl on September 1, 1876. Her final words were, "It's getting dark, wrap the little ones up warm."

She might have gone to her final reward, but it wasn't the last anyone would hear from Kate Miller. The *Pioche Daily Record* reported that the "disembodied spirit" of poor Kate could still be heard and seen at the saloon where she'd breathed her last. For many years afterward, Kate Miller was said to haunt the old red-light district in Eureka.

According to a newspaper article written after her murder, Kate had once been a respectable and hard-working woman who lived in Colorado with her husband and two small children. Fate dealt Kate a harsh blow when another woman fell madly in love with her husband. The problem was that Kate still loved him and had no intention of leaving him. Realizing that she could never have the man of her dreams, the other woman cruelly poisoned his and Kate's two children. The loss was too much for Kate. Grief sent her to the bottle, which broke up her marriage.

Somehow she made her way to Eureka, where she began plying the prostitution trade with other soiled doves in the red-light district. A few years later she gave birth to a third child. There are no extant photographs of Kate in Eureka, or probably elsewhere for that matter, but with a nickname like "Bulldog Kate" it's safe to assume she was not a beauty. Nonetheless, she was able to eke out a living for herself and her child.

On Friday evening, September 1, 1876, Kate staggered half drunk into Cramer's Saloon on North Main Street. She ordered a bottle and kept to herself until "Hog-Eye" Mary Irwin walked in.

Neither woman liked the other. Their enmity was so intense that they ignored one another completely whenever their paths crossed. But tonight would be different. Kate was a mean-tempered drunk.

Under the influence of too many whiskeys she decided it was a good time to insult Mary. So she turned to her and started to yell a string of obscenities at her.

That was the wrong thing to do. Mary was in no mood for the drunken Kate's foul mouth. She glared at her, and then suddenly the women lunged at each other. The fracas spilled out into the street, where Mary pulled a Bowie knife and stabbed Kate several times. When they were finally pulled apart, Kate was mortally wounded. She died in the saloon a short time later and was laid to rest on Monday, September 4, 1876. Mary Irwin was jailed for a few days and then set free after a short hearing on the facts. She left Eureka shortly thereafter.

Kate's sudden, violent, and unexpected death might explain why the ghostly woman would occasionally appear in the area where the saloon once stood.

The Old Courthouse and Hank Parish

The town of Ely is located amid some of the state's most spectacular scenery, including the Great Basin National Park, the Lehman Caves, and the Ward Charcoal Ovens. Whereas now Ely offers a Route 50 respite and access to nature's solitude, it was once a rowdy Wild West town.

On December 12, 1890, Hank Parish became the first man to be legally hanged in Ely. Hank was a man who thought nothing of slaughtering innocent people when they got in his way. Up until the time he walked into Jimmy Curtis's Saloon in Pioche on the night of August 3, 1890, he'd already managed to get away with several murders throughout Nevada. But fate was about to catch up with him. When he stabbed P. G. Thompson for disagreeing with him, Hank brought the wrath of the entire community down on himself. Anyone could see that he wasn't about to get a fair trial in Pioche. So a change of venue was issued and Hank Parish was transferred to Ely. But folks in Ely didn't take kindly to murderous thugs such as Hank. After a two-day trial, it took the jury less than an hour to determine him guilty of first-degree murder.

Dead a hundred years, Hank is said to walk the halls of the old courthouse where he stood trial. At the jail where he awaited his fate, there's plenty of talk about the ghostly goings on of Hank Parish. Some of the workers there are convinced that the ghostly Hank walks the halls of the building. And it would seem that death hasn't improved his disposition. Besides slamming the doors, the ghostly Hank turns the lights on and off and plays with the computers and the telephone.

Railroad Ghosts

The railroads played a vital part in Nevada's history. Cities like Ely, Carlin, Reno, and Las Vegas may not have grown and prospered if not for the railroads. So it's no wonder that some of Nevada's ghosts are connected with the railroad.

Railroading was dangerous work. Accidents were common. The "lucky" railroad employee merely lost a finger, a leg, or an arm. The less fortunate appeared in the next obituary column.

One railroad-associated ghost is that of a young man who has been seen several times in the yards and the museum building at Ely's Railroad Museum. He is believed to be an employee who died in a train accident several years ago. Unexplained cold spots and disembodied voices have been reported in connection with the apparition, who seems to know his way around the yard and building.

The Ely apparition is not the only ghost connected to Nevada's railroads. About the time the moon crests the Ruby Mountains, a spectral conductor steps out of the darkness waving his lantern. Plenty of people around the Carlin area have seen the apparition they call the Ghostly Conductor. No doubt he'll be there forever, swinging his light near the railroad tracks where he lost his life in an accident. One theory holds that the victims of accidents will stay near the area of their deaths in an attempt to prevent others from meeting the same fate. Or perhaps the unfortunate man is so unwilling to give up his job that death is no deterrent to his duties.

Another ghost is that of one of the Chinese immigrants who came to this country in the early 1860s to help build the railroads across California and Nevada. The work these immigrants did was grueling and dangerous. A man who chose to cook for the railroad company seemed assured a somewhat safer job, but that wasn't always so. One night in 1889 a Chinese cook aboard a Nevada, California, and Oregon Railroad dining car got into an argument over his lack of culinary skills. The unfortunate man was murdered when he took offense at insults hurled his way.

Trouble continued when the cook decided that death wasn't going to stop him from attending to his kitchen. One by one, the phantom cook began frightening his former coworkers, especially those who'd taken over his duties as cook. The hauntings got so bad that no one would work in the car for fear the ghostly cook might decide to make an appearance. The railroad had no other choice but to retire the haunted car.

The Commercial Hotel, Tom Horn, and John Coble

John Coble, the manager of the Iron Mountain Ranch in Wyoming, hired the legendary gunman and former lawman Tom Horn in 1901 to protect the ranch's cattle from rustlers. Horn had been instrumental in tracking Geronimo in Arizona; Coble felt he could track rustlers as well.

A friendship developed between the two men that would continue even after Horn was arrested for the murder of Willie Nickell, a fourteen-year-old boy. With the evidence stacked against him, Horn's allies quickly turned from him. John Coble did not. He steadfastly continued to believe in his friend's innocence. In an attempt to help Horn, Coble put up several thousand dollars toward his defense. It was a wonderful gesture, if only Coble had come by the cash honestly. He hadn't. He had stolen the cash from his employer, Frank Bosler. When Bosler discovered Coble's theft, he fired him on the spot.

In the meantime, Tom Horn was found guilty and sentenced to hang. While he awaited his execution, he spent his time weaving the rope that would hang him. On November 20, 1903, he was taken to the gallows and prepared for execution. He sullenly said, "Hurry it up. I got nothing more to say."

Thus Tom Horn was hanged for his crime, one day before his forty-third birthday. His guilt or innocence has been debated ever since. Books have been written about him, and Steve McQueen played Horn in the acclaimed 1980 film *Tom Horn*. Although McQueen did an outstanding job, in true Hollywood style some license was taken with the facts of the story.

Coble, still not without some resources, paid Tom Horn's entire funeral expenses and helped to get his book published. He had done all he could for his friend, and now Coble found himself alone and without a dime to his name. Disheartened, he traveled throughout the West working odd jobs and hoping for better days. They never came. On December 4, 1914 he decided to end his misery. He took pen and paper and wrote the following letter to his wife:

> Elko, Nev., Dec. 4, 1914.
> Dear Elise:
> Believe me, I have tried to pull through. I am ALL IN, I AM ALL IN. Believe me I am yours until the end, and I cannot make good.
> Lovingly,
> [Signature illegible]

His letter written, Coble walked into the lobby of Elko's Commercial Hotel, put his revolver to his head, and pulled the trigger. Why he chose to end his life in this way is a mystery likely never to be solved. He could still be haunting the old hotel to this day. Some employees and patrons believe the place is haunted, and not only by John Coble. Decades after Coble's suicide, a young man caught his cheating wife in the hotel and murdered her as she was leaving her lover's room. The errant wife's apparition is sometimes seen on the floor.

On a note of historical interest, and contrary to what Las Vegas would have us all believe, the Commercial Hotel is where the practice of using live entertainment in casinos began. Back in the 1940s former owner Newt Crumley played a hunch that paid off. He wanted to increase the business, so he hired big-name Hollywood stars to come to his hotel and perform, thereby bringing in the gambling public. Crumley's idea worked so well that Las Vegas and Reno took notice and soon followed suit.

The Ghost Who Demanded Justice

If not for the ghost of Miles Faucett pointing out their crime, Elizabeth and Josiah Potts might have gotten clean away with murder. The sordid tale came to light because of a writer known as Mrs. Brewer. When she and her husband, George, moved from the Lamoille Valley and into the Pottses' former home in Carlin near Elko, they had no idea that a ghost would help them uncover a horrible crime.

Mrs. Brewer wrote a weekly newspaper column under the pen name of "Busy Bee"; she was so pleased with the little four-room house she and her husband owned that she decided to share her happiness with her readers. On January 6, 1889, she wrote the following for the *Elko Free Press*:

> I have been intending to write to you for several weeks, but you know when one moves to a new place one naturally is kept very busy for a while. And in addition to other matters of interest it is a little exciting when one has the good luck to move into a veritable haunted house. Not many persons have such a thing happen to them these days. So far the ghost hasn't scared any of us, but he is here just the same. Sometimes he taps on the headboard of the bed; other times he stalks across the kitchen floor, and anon he hammers away at the door, but nobody's there. But the gayest capers of all are cut up in the cellar. There he holds high revels, and upsets the pickles and carries on generally.

Soon the hauntings got worse. Eventually the noises in the cellar would prove too much for the Brewers. Neither could sleep. Mrs. Brewer asked her husband to go down and find out what was causing the commotion. After a cursory inspection, he called up that everything seemed as it should be. And then, as he turned to climb the steps, he almost tripped over something protruding from the dirt floor. It didn't take much digging for him to realize that it was a bone. Horrified, he brushed away more soil and discovered the grisly remains of a man.

The sheriff was notified of the gruesome discovery; after a look in the dead man's pockets, it was determined that the hacked and charred body belonged to an old rancher named Miles Faucett. Once the unfortunate man's body was removed from the cellar the little house became blissfully quiet. The truth was finally out.

Suspicion quickly fell on the home's previous tenants, Josiah and Elizabeth Potts, who had since moved to Rock Springs, Wyoming. Sheriff Bernard wasn't about to let them escape justice. He wired Wyoming authorities to arrest the pair. The next morning he and Constable J. F. Tiplett went to Rock Springs to bring the Pottses back to Elko.

Elizabeth was the tougher of the two suspects. She maintained a stony composure, but Josiah broke down weeping. He admitted burning and hacking Faucett's lifeless body. But this, he explained, was only after Faucett had shot himself in the head. Both Pottses maintained that Miles Faucett had chosen suicide rather than face public scorn and a possible lynching after having been caught molesting the pair's five-year-old daughter. The only witness to this outrage was Mrs. Potts herself. Apparently no one believed a word she said.

While they awaited trial in the Elko jail, Josiah played solitaire and Elizabeth cursed everyone within earshot. At their trial the couple maintained their innocence and their teenage son testified that he'd seen Faucett put a gun to his own head. This couldn't save Josiah and Elizabeth. On March 21, 1889, Mr. and Mrs. Potts were found guilty of first-degree murder and sentenced to hang. They appealed their death sentences all the way to the Nevada Supreme Court. Even the judge who had presided over their trial asked the Board of Pardons for a commutation of their sentences.

The death sentence was upheld. Two days before her execution, Mrs. Potts tried to cheat the hangman by attempting suicide. She failed.

On June 20, 1890, as the sun shone down on the Ruby Mountains, Josiah and Elizabeth Potts prepared to die. As they made their way to the gallows, they both proclaimed their innocence. After a brief nod to the other, the pair was blindfolded with heavy hoods. Mr. Potts was executed first. Immediately afterward his wife prepared for her departure from this world. According to newspapers the day of her hanging was a hideous affair. Grossly overweight, the murderess's neck was nearly severed by the rope. Witnesses said her white execution dress was covered in crimson.

Back at the Brewers' little house, the strange noises were never heard again. Perhaps the spirit of Mr. Faucett is at last resting in peace.

In 1907 the bodies of Josiah and Elizabeth Potts were disinterred and relocated. The *Elko Free Press* reported:

> The bodies are practically reduced to dust as far as flesh is concerned. The bones too are in an advanced state of decay. The black caps were still over the faces of Mr. and Mrs. Potts. The latter's dress distinctly showed where a quantity of blood flowed over it.

The Potts are buried side by side in an older section of the Elko Cemetery. Their graves are unmarked and only adorned by two bushes that grow wild nearby.

Bibliography

"About Mackay." University of Nevada, Reno: Mackay School of Earth Sciences and Engineering. http://www.unr.edu/mackay/about.

"About St. Mary's Art & Retreat Center: History and Background." St. Mary's Art & Retreat Center. http://stmarysartcenter.org/smacwp/about/.

Alltucker, Ken. "Haunted houses don't spook buyers." *Reno Gazette-Journal*, November 1, 1998.

Ashbaugh, Don. *Nevada's Turbulent Yesterday: A Study in Ghost Towns*. Los Angeles: Westernlore Press, 1963.

Beffort, Brian. "Ghosts rattling around all over the place." *Reno Gazette-Journal*, October 22, 1998.

———. "Nevada hauntings." *Reno Gazette-Journal*, October 31, 1999.

"The Black Book." *Las Vegas Review-Journal*. http://www.reviewjournal.com/business/blackbook/blackbook.info.html.

Cox, Don. "Spooky tales haunt building." *Reno Gazette-Journal*, October 29, 1998.

Delaplane, Gaye. "A Walk Through History." *Reno Gazette-Journal*, June 6, 1999.

De Quille, Dan. *The Big Bonanza*. New York: Alfred A. Knopf, 1947.

Doten, Alfred. *The Journals of Alfred Doten*. Edited by Walter Van Tilburg Clark. 3 vols. Reno: University of Nevada Press, 1973.

Dwyer, Richard A. and Richard E. Lingenfelter. *Dan De Quille, the Washoe Giant: A Biography and Anthology*. Reno: University of Nevada Press, 1990.

Earl, Phillip I. "Ghostly Sightings on Comstock Lode." *Apple Tree*, October 31, 1982.

———. *This Was Nevada*. Reno: Nevada Historical Society, 1986.

———. *This Was Nevada, Volume II: The Comstock Lode*. Reno: Nevada Historical Society, 2000.

Elliott, Russell R. *History of Nevada*. Lincoln: University of Nebraska Press, 1987.

"Famous Cases & Criminals: 'Baby Face' Nelson." Federal Bureau of Investigation. http://www.fbi.gov/about-us/history/famous-cases/baby-face-nelson/bonnie-and-clyde.

Farrell, Ronald A., and Carole Case. *The Black Book and the Mob: The Untold Story of the Control of Nevada's Casinos.* Madison: University of Wisconsin Press, 1995.

"Fatalities at Hoover Dam." U.S. Department of the Interior, Bureau of Reclamation, Lower Colorado Region. http://www.usbr.gov/lc/hooverdam/History/essays/fatal.html.

Frederick, Donna. "Hank the Hanged Ghost Haunts the Annex." *Ely Daily Times*, October 29, 1999.

Hager, Ray. "Mansion clock spooks visitors." *Reno Gazette-Journal*, October 30, 2000.

Hauck, Dennis William. *The National Directory of Haunted Places.* Sacramento: Athanor Press, 1994.

Hegne, Barbara. *The Nevada Vigilante Hangings: Virginia City, Carson City, Dayton, Aurora, "601."* Sparks, NV: Self-published, 2000.

Hickson, Howard. *Mint Mark: "CC"; The Story of the United States Mint at Carson City, Nevada.* Carson City: Nevada State Museum, 1975.

Hillyer, Katherine. *Young Reporter Mark Twain in Virginia City.* Sparks, NV: Western Printing and Publishing, 1964.

"In historic halls, ghostly treads still linger." *Reno Gazette-Journal*, July 11, 1999.

"History." Piper's Opera House. Reprinted from Chic Defrancia, "From the Ashes." *Nevada Magazine* (January/February 2009). http://piperslive.com/history.html.

"James Arthur Champagne." Find a Grave. http://www.findagrave.com/cgi-bin/fg.cgi?page=gr&GSsr=121&GScid=83934&GRid=38122233&.

James, Ronald M. *Temples of Justice: County Courthouses of Nevada.* Reno: University of Nevada Press, 1994.

Lang, Kelly. "Ghost Hunt." *Reno News & Review*, October 28, 1999.

———. "Ghost Story: Four Tales of Terror in Northern Nevada." *Reno News & Review*, October 29, 1997.

McCracken, Robert D. *Tonopah: The Greatest, The Richest and The Best Mining Camp in the World.* Tonopah, NV: Nye County Press, 1990.

Morgan, Dale L. *The Humboldt: Highroad of the West.* New York: Farrar & Rinehart, 1943.

Neilson, Norm. *Tales of Nevada.* Reno: Tales of Nevada Publications, 1994.

Padgett, Sonya. "Luxor Light Serves as Beacon for Millions of Las Vegas Strip Visitors." *Las Vegas Review-Journal*, November 18, 2012. http://www.lvrj.com/living/luxor-light-serves-as-beacon-for-millions-of-strip-visitors-179849021.html.

Paher, Stanley W. *Las Vegas: As it began—As it grew.* Las Vegas: Nevada Publications, 1971.

———. *Nevada Towns & Tales, Volume I: North.* Reno: Nevada Publications, 1981.

Bibliography

Patterson, Edna, Louise A. Ulph, and Victor Goodwin. *Nevada's Northeast Frontier.* Sparks, NV: Western Printing and Publishing, 1969.

"Philip H. Clayton." Find a Grave. http://www.findagrave.com/cgi-bin/fg.cgi?page = gr&GSln = Clayton&GSiman = 1&GScid = 83945&GRid = 9740390&.

Porter, Shirley A. *Goldfield Hotel: But You Can't Leave, Shirley.* San Mateo, CA: Western Book/Journal Press, 1992.

Pryor, Kim. "A real ghost town." *Reno Gazette-Journal*, October 28, 1994.

Reboton, Marge. *Ghosts of the Comstock.* Virginia City, NV: Self-published, 1996.

Ragan, Tom. "City Shuts Down Oasis Motel over Prostitution." *Las Vegas Review-Journal*, November 3, 2012. http://www.lvrj.com/news/city-shuts-down-oasis-motel-over-prostitution-other-allegations-177118751.html.

"Reynolds Grant to Fund Press Foundation Facility." *Las Vegas Review-Journal*, August 19, 2000. http://www.reviewjournal.com/lvrj_home/2000/Aug-19-Sat-2000/business/14203427.html.

Rightmire, Billie J. *Ring Around The Moon.* Minden, NV: Carson Valley Historical Society, 1991.

"Rinckel Mansion." National Park Service: Three Historic Nevada Cities: Carson City, Reno, Virginia City; A National Register of Historic Places Travel Itinerary. http://www.nps.gov/nr/travel/nevada/rin.htm.

Rocha, Guy, and Dennis Myers. "Myth No. 3: Key Pittman on Ice." Nevada State Library and Archives. http://nsla.nevadaculture.org/index.php?option = com_content&task = view&id = 665&Itemid = 418.

Scott E. B. *The Saga of Lake Tahoe.* Antioch, CA: Sierra Tahoe Publishing Co., 1957.

Scrugham, James G. "Fred B. Balzar, Governor 1927–1934." In *Nevada: The Narrative of the Conquest of a Frontier Land* Vol. 1, 555–577. Chicago and New York: The American Historical Society, 1935. Available online at *The Nevada Observer.* http://www.nevadaobserver.com/Reading%20Room%20Documents/Fred%20B.%20Balzer,%20Governor,%201927-1934%20%281935%29.htm.

Shamberger, Hugh A. *The Story of Goldfield.* Carson City: Nevada Historical Press, 1982.

Skorupa, Susan. "Markers of our past." *Reno Gazette-Journal*, October 28, 1997.

Stevens, Joseph E. *Hoover Dam: An American Adventure.* Norman: University of Oklahoma Press, 1988.

Southerland, Cindy. *Cemeteries of Carson City and Carson Valley.* Charleston, SC: Arcadia, 2010.

Stollery, David J., Jr. *Tales of Tahoe.* Sparks, NV: Western Printing & Publishing, 1969.

"Welcome to the Washoe Club." The Washoe Club Haunted Museum. http://www.thewashoeclub.com/.

White, Ken. "Appetizers Column." *Las Vegas Review Journal*, June 19, 1998.
"Woman Commits Suicide Inside Luxor." *Las Vegas Sun*, September 26, 1996. http://www.lasvegassun.com/news/1996/sep/26/woman-commits -suicide-inside-luxor/.
Zanjani, Sally. *Goldfield: The Last Gold Rush on the Western Frontier*. Athens, OH: Ohio University Press/Swallow Press, 1992.
Zauner, Phyllis. *Virginia City: Its History, Its Ghosts*. Sonoma, CA: Zanel Publications, 1994.

About the Author

Photo by Bill Oberding

JANICE OBERDING IS THE AUTHOR OF 13 BOOKS AND LECTURES ON Nevada ghosts and haunted locations. She has also written pieces for the books *Weird Hauntings, Weird Las Vegas and Nevada,* and *Weird Encounters.* She cohosts the popular radio show *Paradacity* on SRNLIVE.COM and has appeared on episodes of the TV shows *Ghost Adventures, Dead Famous, Scariest Places on Earth, Haunted Hotels,* and *Ghost Hunters.*

Other Titles in the

Haunted Series

WWW.STACKPOLEBOOKS.COM • 1-800-732-3669